collaborating to reach a goal. *Dive In* brings this new responsibility to life in a very personal and relevant way. It is a must read for any corporate leader today.

Thomas L. Harrison, Lh.D., Chairman & CEO
Diversified Agency Services Division, Omnicom Group, Inc.

The chance to contribute, to work, to be valued—that's the prize! It's time to open the doors for the full range of human gifts. **Read *Dive In*. It will show you how.**

Timothy P. Shriver, Ph.D., Chairman & CEO, The Special Olympics

In today's highly competitive work environment, a diverse workforce is absolutely essential. Nadine reminds us all that the talent pool must be inclusive of everyone, including those with special needs. What we do as leaders to attract and retain this pool and the extent we're willing to expand our view on what is possible, the better positioned we will be to realize true change. With *Dive In*, **Nadine sets you on the right course! Well done!**

Capt. Ken Barrett, Diversity Director, U.S. Navy

The success of the Civil Rights movement established the ideas of equal opportunity and non-discrimination as fundamental, common values across an otherwise fractious ideological spectrum. We have arrived at a moment of significant opportunity for people with disabilities to make their desire for employment better understood and to draw corrective attention to the barriers they continue to face.

The examples captured in *Dive In: Springboard into the Profitability, Productivity and Potential of the Special Needs Workforce* can **inspire the basis for a more constructive alliance between workforce programs and potential employers**.

Carol Glazer, President, National Organization on Disability

Today's global economy offers unprecedented opportunities to incorporate the talents of all members of our society into the workforce. Organizations that promote a culture of inclusiveness attract, motivate and retain employees based upon their abilities. Vogel's book is **a timely reminder of the importance and benefits of including people with special needs in the labor force.**

Anne C. Ruddy, CCP, CPCU, President, WorldatWork

All businesses, whether a start up or established enterprise, need the right information from the right source at the right time. DIVE IN does just that with comprehensive, just in time information about the special needs workforce delivered by today's leading authority. It's a must read for every entrepreneur, no matter their business.

Susan Wilson Solovic, CEO, co-founder SBTV.com

Nadine Vogel has always been a powerful and compelling voice for the special needs workforce and for the employed parents of special needs children. **With this book, her important wisdom should and will reach far and wide**.

Ellen Galinsky, President, Families and Work Institute

Advance Praise for DIVE IN

Education and technology are the two great equalizers in life, leveling
for everyone, especially the disabled. *Dive In* **provides the informati**
better understand how to remove the barriers to employing 1
segment of the population and in doing so, improve productivity ar

John Chambers, Chairman and CEO, Cisco Systems I

At KPMG, we are committed to an inclusive culture that supports di\
the perspectives and experiences of all our people, including, as D
people with disabilities. Highly skilled, fully engaged, diverse global
organization and are critical to the success of our firm.

John B. Veihmeyer, CEO, KPMG LLP

It is important that all stakeholders, from educators to goverr
private sector employers focus on making the recruitment, hir
of people with disabilities a priority and business objective.
because it's the right or nice thing to do. Just as with other memb
forces, people with disabilities bring new approaches to innovatic
that drive real business improvement. It is also important to cons
an organization's corporate social responsibility efforts that enga\
segment of the workforce will provide. This is why DIVE IN is such ar
anyone in business.

Tig Gilliam, CEO, Adecco Group North America

Great companies take care of their employees—all their employe
written a book that will help companies do a better job at that by (
assumptions about hiring and supporting those who either have
family member with special needs. **Vogel is a leader in her field**

Keith Ferrazzi, CEO, Ferrazzi Greenlight
author of *Who's Got Your Back*

For me, the reason to *Dive In* is quite simple. **Embracing the sp**
nity is the biggest step we can take toward creating a fully h
a fully human workplace is a magnet for customers, colleague\
business practices.

Stephen C. Lundin, Ph.D., author of *FISH! A Ren*
Morale and Improve Results and *CATS: The Nine*
His book *FISH!* was inspired by the special nee

We are clearly in an era where being great means doing good
sible. Means employing people with special needs and allowin\
employee—part of a team with a purpose; a team whose lea

Nadine Vogel is a leader in helping organizations create effective workplaces that include employees who either have a disability or a dependent with special needs. This is a much larger segment of the employee population than many people realize. *Dive In* should be **required reading for anyone with an interest in work/life arena**.

Prof. Brad Harrington, Executive Director, Center for Work & Family, Carroll School of Management, Boston College

Dive In **presents important new as well as proven techniques to advance the employment of people with disabilities**, as presented by Nadine Vogel and some of the most respected disability employers and their leaders, namely IBM's John Evans and McDonald's Kevin Bradley. Lessons imparted are "learn from the best, especially your employees with disabilities" and "don't be afraid to fail a few times to ultimately achieve the culturally complete inclusion of people with disabilities in any and every position in the company." These, among the many lessons, are great for every employer to know.

John D. Kemp, Esq., Executive Director and General Counsel U.S. Business Leadership Network

In these challenging economic times, no competitive advantage can be overlooked. With practical advice and common sense, **Vogel shows us how to tap into the huge untapped talent pool of the special needs workforce.**

Peter Blanck, University Professor & Chairman Burton Blatt Institute, Syracuse University

Dive In illustrates how the interests of businesses, communities and working families who have dependents with special needs intersect in a talent pipeline that when met with understanding, support and collaboration, can almost guarantee success. This book is **a must read for business leaders** across Corporate America."

Donna Klein, President, Corporate Voices for Working Families

Dive In sheds light on the largest minority in the world—the special needs work-force, also the most overlooked segment of the population. Nadine Vogel urges U.S. corporations to open their eyes to these underutilized employees who are well educated, talented, and ready to work. **Hers is a stirring, irrefutable argument not to be missed.**

Carol Evans, President, Working Mother Media, a division of Bonnier Corporation

Small businesses, whether a start up or established enterprise, need the right information from the right source at the right time. *Dive In* does just that with **comprehensive, just in time information about the special needs workforce delivered by today's leading authority.** It's a must read for every entrepreneur, no matter their business.

Susan Wilson Solovic, CEO, co-founder SBTV.com

Practical Books for Smart Professionals from PMP

Dive In

Springboard into the Profitability,
Productivity, and Potential of the
Special Needs Workforce

Nadine O. Vogel

as told to Cindy Brown

Paramount Market Publishing, Inc.

Paramount Market Publishing, Inc.
950 Danby Road, Suite 136
Ithaca, NY 14850
www.paramountbooks.com
Telephone: 607-275-8100; 888-787-8100   Facsimile: 607-275-8101

Publisher: James Madden
Editorial Director: Doris Walsh

Cataloging in Publication Data available
ISBN 978-0-9801745-8-8

Dedication

To my two wonderful daughters Gretchen and Rachel, you have taught me so much and are the inspiration in everything I do and every choice I make. I love you girls!

To my incredibly loving and supportive husband Doug, you are there for me every day and in every way. Only with you by my side is everything possible. I love you more each and every day!

To Grandma Gerty, thank you for teaching me that if it is to be, it's up to me. I miss you very much.

—NADINE O. VOGEL

Contents

Dedication   v

Acknowledgements   xi

Chapter One   Step Up to the Platform—Introduction   1

Chapter Two   Jump Into the Talent Pool—Recruiting   13

Chapter Three   Different Strokes for Different Folks—Training   31

Chapter Four   Supporting the Swimmer—Accommodations   54

Chapter Five   Everyday CPR—Employee Benefits and Benefit Guidance   74

Chapter Six   Gather the Gear—Employee Resources   82

Chapter Seven   Staying Afloat—Work-Life and Support   94

Chapter Eight   Make Waves—The Impact   107

Chapter Nine   Grab Your Towel and Go—Next Steps   117

Appendix: Organizations, Resources, and Websites   120

Index   128

The Authors   131

Acknowledgements

FOR THIS BOOK I have to thank my husband, Doug. His love, support and patience is what allows me to do all I do. I wake every day knowing how lucky I am to have married him over 24 years ago. I also have to thank my girls, Gretchen and Rachel, who are the true inspiration for this book. They continuously help me to maintain perspective and never let me forget that no matter how successful I may become in business, I am first and foremost their mom.

I also must thank my co-writer, Cindy Brown, for without her incredible flexibility, humor, insight, and skill this book would have never come to fruition. I am fortunate to work with her and be able to consider her my friend.

To my Springboard Dream Team, Steve Cody, Bill Dueease, Meryl Kaplan, and James Barrood, thank you for listening and sharing your collective expertise.

Chandra Vick, who is not only my attorney, but also someone I must thank for letting me bend her ear whenever the mood strikes and for her extraordinary ability to make sure every contract is just as it should be.

Finally, I would like to thank everyone who gave up precious time to be interviewed for this book. I am grateful for their willingness to openly share their companies' best practices along with their own personal insights in supporting the special needs workforce. It is their words that will truly make this book a success.

NADINE O. VOGEL
JUNE 2009

M ANY THANKS to Sally Marks for her wonderful feedback, her continual encouragement, and her boundless optimism.

CINDY BROWN
JUNE 2009

CHAPTER ONE
Step Up to the Platform — Introduction

IMAGINE, for a moment, your perfect workforce. *Good* employees would possess the education and skills needed for your company's particular jobs and positions, but what other traits would *perfect* employees exhibit? See if your list of qualities matches mine:

+ They'd be dedicated—to hard work, to specific projects, and to my company.

+ They'd be productive, performing quality work that others want to emulate.

+ They'd have an out-of-the-box perspective; plus an ability to creatively troubleshoot problems, discover and seize opportunities, and innovate solutions to issues I hadn't even considered yet.

+ They'd be there when I need them. Absenteeism would not be an issue.

+ They'd stay for years and years, fanning the flame of loyalty, and passing the torch of institutional knowledge to whomever needed it next.

+ As a bonus, my perfect workforce would elevate the status of my company. Clients would actually do more business with me, and think better of my company because I'd hired these employees.

Add a few qualities to my list, if you'd like, and then hold in your mind that image of your perfect workforce. Wouldn't you like to find and hire those employees? Wouldn't you want to hold on to them once you found them? Wouldn't you want to create an environment in which your perfect employees felt welcome, included, and valued?

Read on, and you'll acquire the tools and find the inspiration to do just that. You'll learn where (and how) to recruit great employees, how to create a supportive, inclusive business environment that will keep them happy and productive, and how to retain those workers for years. Which workers? Who, exactly, are these great employees? They're people with disabilities, parents of children with special needs, and older workers—the special needs workforce.

This workforce embodies all of the qualities that I listed above. Consider these study-confirmed facts:

- People with disabilities are more likely to stay with an employer than their non-disabled counterparts. Older workers also have reduced turnover rates.

- People with disabilities consistently meet or exceed job performance and productivity expectations.

- People with disabilities have a well-deserved reputation (backed up by research) for innovation. Accustomed to adapting to a variety of situations, they are often quick to troubleshoot, formulate new ideas, and adopt cutting-edge solutions.

- Absentee rates are lower for people with disabilities and for older workers compared with "typical" employees.

Also, anecdotal evidence indicates that including people with disabilities in the workplace improves morale and worker productivity. These facts play out in work arenas all over the world. Suzanne Colbert, chief executive officer of the Australian Employers Network of Disability, commented that recent research found that, "organizations that successfully include people with disability gain significant benefits, including lower staff turnover, fewer workplace injuries, reduced absenteeism, and increased workplace morale."

⊃ **Surprising Statistics: Loyalty and Reduced Turnover**

In an article in *Fortune* magazine, Pizza Hut stated that the turnover rate in its Jobs Plus™ Program (geared toward people with cognitive disabilities) was **20 percent, compared with a 150 percent turnover rate among employees without disabilities.** In the same article, Carolina Fine Snacks, Greensboro, North Carolina, reported that since hiring people with disabilities, employee turnover dropped from 80 percent every six months to less than 5 percent.

A tasty bonus for Carolina Fine Snacks: productivity rose from 70 percent to 95 percent; absenteeism dropped from 20 percent to less than 5 percent; and tardiness dropped from 30 percent to zero.

Let's not forget the "bonus" quality I listed earlier; "I'd like my perfect workforce to elevate the status of my company." The special needs workforce can do that, too.

A national survey reported that 92 percent of American consumers view companies that hire people with disabilities more favorably than those that do not. And, 87 percent of the public would prefer to give their business to companies that hire people with disabilities.

And don't forget that by hiring the special needs workforce, you are also marketing to them. Check out these numbers:

+ The U.S. Census reports that people with disabilities and their network (family and friends) represent $1 trillion in discretionary spending.

+ By themselves, adults with disabilities spend $200 billion, twice that of the teen market, and 17 times that of the "tweens."

+ Parents of children with special needs have the same income, assets, and homeownership levels as the general population.

+ The "fifty-plus" market is the most affluent age segment. It spends
more than $1 trillion on goods and services.

Convinced Yet?

It's okay if you're not convinced of the potential of the special needs workforce quite yet; there's a whole book ahead. I encourage you to read it from
beginning to end, not skipping over chapters, because only by reading each
chapter will you begin to see the whole picture, the great opportunity that
exists for your company, and the way in which all of the pieces connect to
create an environment that will truly welcome this particular workforce.

I coined the term "special needs workforce" to include more than just the
group of people with disabilities, but also people who care for dependents
with special needs, and older workers with impairments. Let's take a brief
look at these groups:

People with disabilities

One of the most overlooked segments of the American population,
this group is the largest minority in the world. It includes people with
physical impairments like blindness, deafness, or paraplegia, and cognitive impairments like learning disabilities, traumatic brain injury, or
Down Syndrome. There are more American with disabilities than there
are Canadians, with or without disabilities. Many of the people in this
enormous talent pool are well-educated, talented, and ready to work,
though widely under-used.

People who care for dependents with special needs

This group is mostly comprised of parents of children with special
needs. Approximately 23 million Americans have at least one child
(aged 5 to 16) with special needs. Add those with children younger
than age 5, or older than age 16, or both and the number grows. This

group also includes people who may be caring for a dependent with a disability, perhaps a sibling or a spouse. The group can be enlarged again to consider those who care for aging parents. Something to consider: some of these caregivers may be caring for more than one dependent. A 2005 Pew Research Center survey found that approximately 13 percent of Americans aged 49 to 59 currently care for their children and aging parents at the same time.

Older workers with impairments

This is a tough group to nail down. Many older workers do not disclose disabilities or impairments, fearing that employers may see them as "too old" for their jobs. Others may not even admit their impairments to themselves, or consider their impairment as "just a part of life," rather than a disability. For these reasons, they are typically not included in the number of people with disabilities, though their numbers are certainly great.

⮑ Surprising Statistics: Older Workers

Studies indicate that:

- Older employees, as a result of their experience, make better on-the-spot judgments and complete tasks more accurately than do their younger peers.
- Total sick days for older workers are lower than for any other age group.
- Older workers express more loyalty to their employers than do younger workers.
- An individual's interpersonal skills and implicit knowledge improve or remain stable until late in life.
- Older workers consistently meet or exceed job performance and productivity expectations.

"But why does *my company* need them?"

I'm often approached by people who say, "I understand that this is a large market. I understand that more and more people with disabilities are educated. Even knowing that, why is it so important that I focus on people with disabilities?"

Surfing the Silver Tsunami

To begin with, you're going to need the special needs workforce. Our nation is aging, and the wave of retirees from the baby boom generation is gaining momentum. The Population Reference Bureau (PRB) predicts that by 2030, about one-fifth of the U.S. population will be older than 65 and the Department of Labor estimates that, by 2014, thirty-six million employees will leave their jobs. The baby boomers are retiring.

In a 2006 study by the Society for Human Resource Managers (SHRM), human resource professionals listed the upcoming demographic shift as one of the most critical issues facing employers, citing the implications for leadership and knowledge retention.

"But wait," you say, "that was 2006. Things have changed since then." It's true, things have changed, and it may be that more people decide to stay in their positions for financial reasons. Some also believe that globalization will help to offset the retirement wave. Maybe, maybe not. It would be wise to consider the fact that the United States' population is not the only one that's aging. Europe and Japan expect the largest increases in their elderly populations.

Let's say, for the sake of argument, that the silver tsunami turns out to be just a good-sized swell—a "sneaker wave." Are you familiar with those? They're big waves that, yes, "sneak" up on you, and can carry you out to sea. Warnings posted along beaches known for these waves advise against turning your back to the sea. Don't turn your back on this wave, either; prepare for it. Let's say that your valuable older workers stay in the workforce; in order to keep them, and to keep them working productively, you will need to support them, perhaps by accommodating impairments that often accompany aging. According to an Association of American Retired Persons (AARP) study, nearly 70 percent of people over age fifty will be dealing with some sort of disability in their lifetime. Support them, and you'll keep them.

More Than You Know

And here's a great perk—supporting older workers and people with disabilities helps you to support other employees, not just the 15 percent with disability-related issues that you already employ. Bet I caught your attention there. Let me say it again: *the 15 percent of employees with disability-related issues that you already employ.* Most organizations have no idea that their workforce is already comprised so heavily of people with disabilities (6 percent) and parents of children with special needs (9 percent). The number may not be obvious, perhaps because people haven't disclosed their disabilities or opened up about their parenting situations. Once these folks see that you are supporting employees with similar issues, they may feel more comfortable in asking for assistance.

> ### Tax Benefits for Businesses Who Have Employees with Disabilities
>
> The U.S. Internal Revenue Service offers some tax credits and deductions for businesses that employ people with disabilities. Some benefits are offered only to small businesses, others to businesses regardless of size. Check out the IRS website at www.irs.gov/businesses/small/article/0,,id=185704,00.html for more information.

You're also going to find yourself with another group of valued employees who will need your support—those who become disabled while working for you. Not only can anyone become disabled at any time, but the majority of disabilities are acquired during adulthood. According to the

2000 National Organization on Disability/Harris Survey of Americans with Disabilities, only 24 percent of people with disabilities surveyed acquired those impairments before age nineteen. I'm happy to do the math for you: that means, on average, 76 percent of disabilities are acquired after age twenty—during the time when a person is most likely to be employed. Don't you want to retain your great employees, who suddenly (or not so suddenly) find themselves disabled?

The logic follows that if you support your employees, you'll also retain them, thereby reducing turnover—another impact to your bottom line. According to the American Management Association, turnover-related expenditures can cost up to 150 percent of an experienced worker's annual salary. Are you beginning to connect the dots? Support equals productivity and retention, both of which ultimately impact your company's profit-ability.

Becoming a Employer of Choice

But let's not stop there. Support and flexibility are key components of being an employer of choice. Actively supporting these values shows a respect for work-life balance. Ah, there's a buzz word: "work-life balance." Google that term and you'll pull up hundreds of thousands of results including articles, books, and websites, all touting work-life balance. You might note that the new first family is mentioned in several sites—yep, even the President and First Lady recognize the importance of balancing work and family. They're not alone. Surveys show that Gen Xers and Gen Ys (the hot new talent you need) both value this balance, to the point where they will quit (or not accept) jobs that interfere with their family and off-work life. According to the SHRM study mentioned previously, work-life balance is the second most important societal trend. It's no flash in the pan, either. It's expected to be a career-long concern for Generations X and Y, and will become increasingly important as couples have children later in life, and as people find themselves caring for aging parents. To become an employer of choice, you're going to have to shine when it comes to work-life issues.

The Diversity-Innovation Equation

Diversity also plays a part in being an employer of choice; it's one of the top considerations for prospective employees. As diversity professionals know, it can do more than that; it can breed innovation. People with diverse backgrounds, experiences, and ways of thinking can positively change your products, your services, even your company. You may notice that I'm using the word "can." Yes, these people can innovate, they can impact your business, they can put you ahead of the competition, but there's more to the equation. I like to say, "Diversity plus inclusion equals innovation." "Plus inclusion?" you may ask. "Doesn't 'diversity' mean inclusion?" Not necessarily. Let's say your company hires a young man with a disability, but that your company culture prevents him from feeling included. He may turn out to be a good employee, but is he going to come to you with his great new ideas? Probably not. People first have to feel included, welcomed, and comfortable; only then will they risk being innovative.

Truly Diverse

For some reason, people with disabilities are often omitted from the diversity discussion. It's strange, since they fit the definition of diversity in many ways. How? First of all, people with disabilities come from all walks of life. Advocates are fond of saying that the disability community is the "only equal opportunity minority"—the only one where anyone can join at any time. It's also the only minority that is inclusive of people of every race, creed, culture, and gender.

In addition, individuals with disabilities have great diversity of experience, dealing with situations that "typical" people never face. Most of us, when faced with a flight of stairs, don't have to wonder how we're getting to the top. We don't have to wonder, when presented with a video, how we're going to know what's being shown, or said, on screen. People with disabilities often have unique experiences and creative solutions that they can bring to your company table, as do the parents of children with special needs, who are used to troubleshooting, and older workers, who have years of experience under their belts.

Wait, we're not done yet. There's also diversity within disability. There are the obvious differences: some people are blind, some people are deaf, and so on. Then there's the not-so-obvious diversity within even specific disabilities. For example, people lose their sight at all different ages, from birth to old age. That not only changes their experience of the world, but also changes the means they use to experience it. People who become blind at a younger age might learn and use Braille (as well as technological advances like screen readers), whereas people who lose their vision later often learn just enough Braille to get by, or never use it all.

There's more. Let's continue to use the example of people with vision impairment. Some may see the world as through a filmy cloth, others may have "holes" in their field of vision, and yet others may only be able to sense light and dark. The fact that they experience the world in such obviously different ways may help us (and our companies) to understand that everyone sees the world through different lenses.

These diverse life experiences can contribute to diversity of thought, which can lead to innovation, *but only through inclusion*. It's such an important piece of the success puzzle that Corporate America, realizing that diversity just isn't enough, is slowly shifting toward diversity *and* inclusion initiatives, and diversity *and* inclusion departments.

The Springboard of Diversity and Inclusion

That's the platform for this book—that disability is an integral part of diversity, and that for diversity to truly work, you must have inclusion as well. Like any platform, that's just a jumping-off place. Once you dive into this book, you'll find a sea of information and inspiration. You'll get advice regarding best practices, from myself, from leading experts in the field of disability and aging, and from America's in-the-know corporations:

+ Adecco, the largest human capital solutions company in the world, shares some of its secrets for recruiting people with disabilities.

+ Kaiser Permanente explains how it retains good employees and increases the productivity of current workers.

+ Accounting giant KPMG reveals how its disability-related affinity groups create work-life balance.

+ McDonald's demonstrates the ways it practices inclusion.

+ These companies value and actively seek out the special needs workforce. They and other leading corporations understand the value of this workforce, and so graciously contributed to this book, hoping to inspire others. As you read on, you'll hear stories from:

  – Adecco

  – Cisco

  – CVS

  – Ernst & Young

  – IBM

  – Kaiser Permanente

  – KPMG

  – McDonald's

  – Microsoft

  – Proctor & Gamble

  – Starbucks

  – Walgreens

  – WalMart

As consultant to some of these organizations, I've joined them on their paths to success. Some of them have been walking this road for a long time

(IBM hired its first employee with a disability in 1914), while others are just now clearing a trail, but all of their experiences, and mine, will help you to create a workplace and a culture that will appropriately support the special needs workforce and do so successfully.

My co-author and I also play other roles in the world of disability, roles that are reflected in this book. I understand the needs of working parents of children with special needs, as my two beautiful girls have disabilities. My co-author, Cindy Brown, who lives with Ehlers-Danlos Syndrome, offers the perspective of someone with a physical disability, as well as someone who works in the access/Americans with Disabilities Act (ADA) arena. That said, though both of us are knowledgeable about the ADA, we do not write from a legal perspective. There are many wonderful government documents that provide information about compliance. This book, written from a social justice perspective, instead promotes diversity and inclusion, and illustrates how the special needs workforce can positively impact your bottom line. *Dive In* is not a stick, but a big, juicy carrot.

CHAPTER TWO

Jump into the Talent Pool — Recruiting

BEFORE JUMPING into anything, it's wise to look before you leap. Check out the current of the river, the placement of the rocks, or the depth of the pool. Decide whether it's better to jump in feet first, or dive in headlong. You may even want to make sure you have the right equipment for a specialized dive. And if you're like me, you'll first have to decide, "Is it worth it?" You'll most likely need to weigh the advantages of diving into an unknown pool. Is it really better than staying in a nice, safe place?

When you're considering a dive into the untapped talent pool of the special needs workforce, the answer is an unequivocal "yes." Why? Fifty-four million American adults, plus another 23 million parents of children with special needs—that's 77 million Americans. That's only a partial answer to the question, "Why recruit the special needs workforce?" but we'll start there.

Big Numbers, Big Potential

From just a numbers perspective, the statistics are staggering. Around 54 million American adults identify themselves as disabled, and another 23 million are parents who have at least one child aged 5 to 16 with special needs. But experts agree that there are even more people with impairments or disability-related issues, who do not identify as such—e.g., people who may have acquired a hearing loss, but don't consider themselves hard-of-hearing. People with age-related impairments seldom identify themselves as having a disability. Others may find that medical technology, like cochlear implants or some of the amazing prosthetics now available, lessens the impact of their impairments so much that they don't consider themselves disabled. Still others may be loath to disclose a hidden disability, fearing discrimination.

There's more—the numbers I've quoted most likely don't include the 2.9 million veterans with disabilities, including more than 180,000 from the recent war on terrorism. Talk about a pool of dedicated workers. Besides their loyalty and strong work ethic, many of these folks have the education, training, and skills that could really benefit your company.

➲ Positive Perspectives:
An Essential Part of the American Workforce

"Americans with disabilities are an essential and underutilized part of our workforce. Fairness is important, but providing you with the supports and services so you can succeed goes beyond that—it goes to the heart of our nation's future. Because in an era of intense global competition, we can't afford not to put everyone to work."

—President Barack Obama, in a speech given in honor of Disability Employment Awareness Month, 2008

True to his word, President Obama has pledged to issue an executive order that mandates the hiring of an additional 100,000 federal employees with disabilities over the next five years.

Now, look at those numbers, and realize that by the time this book is published, those numbers will have grown exponentially. The population of people with disabilities increases every day. Why? Better medical technology means that more and more people survive accidents (or acts of war). Increased medical knowledge also means that people are living longer, and with age comes a higher prevalence of disability. As time goes by, you're going to see more and more people with disabilities.

You're also going to see an older population, as baby boomers begin to age. "I start by saying corporations have no option when it comes to considering people with disabilities and older workers, primarily because society, and therefore the workforce, is evolving in that direction," says Dr. Percil Stanford, Senior Vice President and Chief Diversity Officer for AARP. "It's imperative that corporations and Human Resource professionals look seriously at the total workforce. If they're doing their jobs and looking forward, they'll see the underlying connections. They have to be much more global and inclusive in their thinking." Older workers and people with disabilities will probably make up a large percentage of the population; shouldn't they be a large part of your workforce?

> **Positive Perspectives: Older Workers**

Both Adecco and CVS Caremark proactively recruit older workers. Adecco's Renaissance Program enlightens older workers regarding temporary employment opportunities and benefits. Employees have access to health and prescription benefits, as well as a bit more income and activity in their lives.

Today, more than 18 percent of CVS Caremark's workforce is over age fifty. "They're dedicated to the job, have great customer service skills, and are adaptable and dependable," says Stephen M. Wing, Director of Workforce Initiatives for CVS Caremark. He provides an example: "An employee who was in his seventies was helping to unload delivery trucks one day when someone said to him, 'You don't have to do that.' 'No, no,' he replied, 'I'm part of the team here.'"

Numbers and percentages are just one reason your workforce should reflect society. "As people come into our stores, they want to see people who look like them," says Stephen M. Wing, Director of Workforce Initiatives for CVS Caremark. Kevin Bradley, Director of Diversity Initiatives for McDonald's, agrees. "Consumers get excited when they see someone like them behind the counter," he says.

The value of the special needs workforce extends beyond the consumer market. Did you know that by hiring this population you're also making your company more attractive to the hot young talent that everyone wants? A recent study found that 78 percent of young people (aged 14 to 18) said money was less important than personal fulfillment. Another 10 percent identified themselves as "ethical enthusiasts" who are more concerned about the values of their potential employer than they are about starting pay. And, you guessed it; one of the values that ranks high among young job seekers is *diversity*.

> ### ⟳ Inspiration & Innovation: Not Why?, but Why Not?
>
> *"'Why recruit people with disabilities?' We get that question all the time. A greater question is, 'Why wouldn't you?' We hire people of color, and of different ethnicities. Diversity is a critical part of a good strategic long-term business model. It's just the right thing to do. It's often a challenge to get past the perception that hiring people with disabilities is somehow a great and charitable act that requires a giant investment, or that having a person with a disability around is a whole lot of work, with not a lot of return. We know that's not true. Disabusing people of that myth is probably the number one issue."*
>
> —John Evans, IBM Human Ability and Accessibility Center, IBM

Creativity and Common Sense

Remember my diversity–innovation equation from the last chapter? I strongly believe (and I am not alone in this belief) that people with diverse backgrounds, experiences, and ways of thinking can positively change your products, your services, even your company. I also believe that the special needs workforce may be even more innovative than "typical" folks. Why? We often have to think out of the box in order to get what we need for ourselves or our children. Whether it's healthcare or daycare, accommodations for work or for school, or transportation dilemmas, we often have to come up with creative solutions to everyday situations. "People with disabilities are no different in bringing particular skills and abilities to the table," say Shelley Kaplan, Director of the Southeast Disability Business Technical Assistance Center (DBTAC). "But because of the nature of disability, sometimes they can brainstorm a challenging situation better than the average worker. For example, we had a technical assistance specialist who answered our hotline. He had no functional use of his extremities. To answer the phone, he rigged up a switch on his power chair. When he moved it with his finger, it would lift the phone off the receiver, automatically place the call in hands-free mode, and he could answer it. It was a low-cost and one-of-a-kind accommodation." Pretty innovative, wouldn't you say?

Inspiration & Innovation: Adecco's Athlete Career Program

Where do athletes go after the Olympics and Paralympics? Many go to work. Recognizing the dedication and persistence of these athletes, Adecco created a tailor-made program that helps them transfer skills from sports to careers. Available in thirty countries worldwide, the Athlete Career Program offers career planning, job placement assistance, and educational, and training programs to Olympians, Paralympians, and hopefuls.

"People with disabilities have to innovate all the time," says Bonnie St. John, a Paralympic gold medalist downhill skier. "We have to assess the environment, process the equipment, and figure out how we're going to get things done." She should know. Bonnie decided to take up skiing at a time when there had never been any medalists who were African American (as she is). Never before had someone with one leg trained full-time at a ski-racing academy. And to top it all off, she lived in snowless San Diego.

None of these things phased Bonnie. "As people with disabilities, we have to make things happen," she says. She also believes that this type of innovation and initiative paves the way for success in today's world. "Though people often use sports as a metaphor in business, I think that disabled sports is a better metaphor for the world of work today. Athletes with disabilities, rather than being recruited as young talent, have to take initiative. They may have to build their own customized equipment, or even hire their own coaches," says Bonnie. "This translates into the world of work. I know a person who is blind, and was a Paralympic medalist in judo. He's now a sales manager for the Hartford. Since he can't drive, he had to come up with another way to cover his territory. He decided to ride along with his sales representatives. Most managers probably do ride-alongs from time to time, but he gets to spend a lot more time with his reps. It's become one of the reasons for his success."

⊃ **Inspiration & Innovation: Out-of-the-Chute Innovation**

Cognitive disabilities often carry with them a greater stigma than do mobility and sensory disabilities. Too often overlooked is the great potential for innovation *because* of different thinking and learning styles. Animal scientist Dr. Temple Grandin, for instance, is deservedly famous for designing more humane livestock handling processes. Nicknamed "the woman who thinks like a cow" by a documentary filmmaker, Dr. Grandin believes that she understands animals because she is primarily a visual thinker with an incredible ability to recall detail—a result of her autism.

"Now," you may argue, "those people are exceptional. They're Paralympic athletes, for heaven's sake!" True. I'm not trying to say that people with disabilities are all exceptional—in fact, the disability community finds that generalization offensive. But what I do believe is that many people with disabilities, in order to be successful, have to go an extra distance. Deborah Dagit, Vice President and Chief Diversity Officer at Merck & Co. is one such person. "When I was in college, I applied to work at a photo kiosk. I had a cast on my leg at the time, and was using crutches. When I met with them, I could tell there was no way they would hire me. I said, 'I'll work for three days for free. If I do well, you have to give me the job.'" Deb's initiative and her persistence landed her that job.

That persistence translates into a strong work ethic as well. Employees with disabilities stay with employers for longer lengths of time, and have fewer absences. I think that last fact is worth re-stating—they have fewer absences. I was speaking with an executive at a large retail firm who employed a number of people with disabilities. When I asked him how it was going, he said, "Okay, except for snow days." "Oh," I thought to myself, "it's probably tough for people with disabilities to get around in the snow, or maybe they have transportation issues . . ." "Yeah," he said. "All of my other employees call in, but the folks with disabilities show up, so I have to open the store."

Christine M. Peterson, PHR, Branch Manager, Adecco, relates another story of employee loyalty:

> *"Rebecca Southerland has been battling a rare form of Thyroid Cancer for 11 years. Though she is receiving treatment at John Hopkins University, is hooked up to all this machinery, and has an entire case of medication that she travels with at all times, she still shows up to work every day that she is scheduled, is always on time, and never complains. She works extremely hard, and is always pleasant and helpful to others. This is so powerful because we work in a temporary industry that often requires patience and flexibility, as associates often get called out at the last minute. Rebecca, who has every excuse to quit, be late, or not show up, has a work ethic that we can all learn from."*

Older workers, another segment of the special needs workforce, have also been shown to have more company loyalty than "typical workers." "I think that some people, as they progress in life, have made decisions about what's important," says AARP's Dr. Percil Stanford. "Work quite often becomes a value that is much more prevalent as people age. When we're younger, it's often a means to survive. As we age, many of us take more pride and commitment in what we do. We want to leave something behind, to say, "I helped to build that building, or set up that data system. I made a difference."

These folks—older workers, people with disabilities, and parents of children with special needs—can make a difference to your company and to your bottom line. Stephen M. Wing of CVS Caremark believes that hiring the special needs workforce is a "Blue Ocean Strategy." This strategy, identified by W. Chan Kim and Renée Mauborgne, suggests that companies, rather than competing over known market space (or known talent) look for "blue ocean"—deeper, wider, as yet unexplored space. "It's a good business model, very competitive," says Mr. Wing. "We believe that working with people with disabilities is like sitting in clear blue water, with no one else around us. It gives us a competitive advantage."

> ⤵ **Positive Perspectives:** A No-Brainer
>
> *"I think companies fail to realize that 80 to 85 percent of disabilities are a result of some life event. So many people still have tremendous skills. We see the disability community as an untapped resource for talent. It's a no-brainer."*
>
> —William Rolack, Diversity Manager, Adecco

Where to Dive?

Now that you've decided to jump into this clear blue ocean—what next? Or should I say, "Where next?" One of the chief complaints I hear is that people don't know where to find this talent. Let me point you toward another no-brainer idea: partner with disability organizations. The concept is so simple that I could stop there, but I'd like to show you just how simple—and how successful—these partnerships can be.

You may contribute to disability-related organizations, or volunteer for them. But think for a moment about these non-profits and government organizations; their missions (generally speaking) are to support people with disabilities. How better to support people than by giving them employment options and opportunities? That's where these organizations line up with your aim of recruiting people with disabilities.

Take a cue from the three largest employers in the U.S.—the federal government, WalMart, and Adecco. *All* of them partner with disability organizations. Adecco, the leading global personnel service provider, is so committed to partnering with disability organizations that its annual disability-specific diversity accomplishment report, *Disability Recruitment*

Partnerships, Events and Activities, contains nineteen pages of information about Adecco's partnerships (*nineteen* pages!). It lists partners along with specific recruiting events and programs, as well as accolades it has received as a result of these partnerships (hmm . . . kind of goes back to that public perception piece, doesn't it?).

As part of its partnership with Abilities, Inc./Business Advisory Council, Adecco colleagues volunteer, offer job shadowing, and participate in bi-monthly practice interviews with students seeking opportunities in the New York market. "Sometimes we also have reverse interviews, where the consumers interview us," says William Rolack, Diversity Manager for Adecco. "It gives us a chance to see their perspective, to look at things from the other side of the table."

Besides providing Adecco with that valuable feedback and a pool of ready-to-work talent, Abilities, Inc. has also helped Adecco evaluate the accessibility of its applicant testing and registration process.

⇨ Inspiration & Innovation: Creating Opportunity

In 2002, Walgreens' Senior Vice President Randy Lewis had an idea. Since the company was investing in new technology to make distribution more efficient, why not create opportunities for people with disabilities? Walgreens intentionally used universal design concepts to design and create new equipment, partnered with agencies that provided employment services to people with disabilities, and created training opportunities for the new managers to help insure an inclusive workplace. Now, two Walgreens distribution centers, (one in Anderson, South Carolina, and a new one in Windsor, Connecticut) have exceeded their employment goals: people with disabilities comprise more than 33 percent of the workforce in both centers.

Walgreens, another leader in disability employment, strongly relies on its partnerships. "We never recruited for special groups," says Deb Russell, Manager of Outreach and Employee Services for Walgreens. "Instead, we created partnerships with organizations like vocational rehabilitation and DD (Developmental Disability) agencies, and educated them about our jobs." Like Adecco, Walgreens' partners also helped them to make its application process more accessible. "We rewrote some of the interview process, adding more guidelines for the interviewer. Now, if someone is struggling with a question, the interviewer has different options and different questions, so that the applicant can find another way to answer."

Disability organizations can also provide virtual support in the form of websites and listservs. WalMart, along with many other large companies, posts employment ads on disability-related websites. Listservs cross the country, and indeed, the world. These virtual postings not only help you to recruit; they let the world know that you are looking for diverse talent, and that you support the special needs workforce.

Diving Partners

I could fill an entire book with lists of disability organizations and government agencies that can help your company recruit the special needs workforce. A very few are discussed here. More are listed in the appendix at the end of this book, but neither list is exhaustive. There are literally hundreds of organizations—global, national, and local—that can help you in your recruiting efforts. The key is knowing which organizations are the right partners for you, your company, and your employees. Different nonprofits have different strengths and focuses. To get you started, here is a small sample of organizations you can contact:

The Office of Disability Employment (ODEP)
866-633-7365   www.dol.gov/odep

This sub-cabinet level policy agency in the Department of Labor offers resources to both employers and job-seekers. It provides links to job-matching and job-posting sites, offers tips for conducting an accessible interview process, and specialized recruiting tools and programs, like:

The Employer Assistance Referral Network (EARN)
866-EARN NOW (866-327-6669)   www.earnworks.com

ODEP's toll-free telephone and electronic information referral service can help you locate and recruit qualified workers with disabilities. EARN's technical assistance specialists will even take job orders, seek out qualified local candidates, and present you with the information.

The Workforce Recruitment Program for College Students with Disabilities (WRP)
202-693-7880
www.wrpjobs.com or www.dol.gov/odep/programs/workforc.htm

Looking for a qualified, highly-motivated college grad? This ODEP program provides a free nation-wide database of pre-screened graduating students with disabilities who are looking for both permanent and temporary positions.

State Vocational Rehabilitation Agencies
(There are various lists of these agencies; Search on "State Vocational Rehabilitation Agencies" for a national list, or add your state to the search in order to find local services.)

A great local pipeline for recruits, these state-supported agencies help individuals with disabilities to find and secure gainful employment commensurate with their abilities and capabilities. By offering training and other support services, they help people to hone the skills that allow them to return to work, to enter a new line of work, or to enter the workforce for the first time.

⮑ **Surprising Statistics: One in Four Vets . . .**

An estimated one in four soldiers returns home from Iraq and Afghanistan with a service-related injury.

HireVetsFirst.gov lists ten reasons to hire veterans, disabled or not:

1. An accelerated learning curve

2. Leadership

3. Teamwork

4. Diversity and inclusion in action

5. Efficient performance under pressure

6. Respect for procedures

7. Technology and globalization

8. Integrity

9. Conscious of health and safety standards

10. Triumph over adversity

Connect with this great workforce at www.HireVetsFirst.gov, or HireHeroesUSA.org

The U.S. Business Leadership Network (USBLN)
www.usbln.org

The only national disability organization led by business for business, USBLN supports development and expansion of 53 BLN affiliates in 31 states. These organizations recognize and promote best practices in hiring, retaining, and marketing to people with disabilities. Using a business-to-business approach, they provide career fairs, mentoring, and internship programs, as well as training programs for employers. Many of the employers interviewed for this book are members.

Easter Seals
800-221-6827, 312-726-4258 TTY*
www.easterseals.com

*TTYs (TeleTYpewriters) are used by some people who have difficulty hearing or speaking and cannot easily use a typical telephone.

Easter Seals offers a variety of workforce development services for job-seekers with disabilities, including special programs for older workers and returning veterans with disabilities. Job readiness training focuses on workplace and career management skills. Job placement services not only connect workers and businesses, but in some cases offer continuing on-the-job support or assistance in fulfilling job responsibilities. Some Easter Seals locations also provide occupational and industry-based skills training, and assistive technology services.

The American Association of People with Disabilities (AAPD)
800-840-8844 V/TTY   www.aapd.com

As the country's largest cross-disability membership organization, AAPD can provide a vast array of information and resources. "We work very closely with AAPD," says John Evans of IBM's Human Ability and Accessibility Center. "They help us to get an overview of the disability community. We don't just want feedback about our strategies; we want to know what they're advocating for, and what their strategies might be." WalMart has also benefited from this connection. "Realizing the importance of connecting to the disability community, we reached out to AAPD. They've given us amazing insights into what we could do to improve our programs," says Crosby Cromwell, Manager of Disability Markets for WalMart.

WalMart also participates in Disability Mentoring Day, an AAPD–hosted effort that connects job-seekers with disabilities with employers. Recognized nationally on the third Wednesday of every October, this coordinated effort promotes career development through hands-on career exploration, on-site job shadowing, and ongoing mentoring. Not only can this experience help your company find recruits, but it also provides a connection to your community, and an opportunity for inclusion. "Employers should get involved in Disability Mentoring Day," says the Southeast DBTAC's Shelley Kaplan. "There's nothing like firsthand experience to remove the 'you, us, and them' mentality."

A Tale of Two Internships

The first–hand experience provided by mentoring and internships also illuminates the individuality and various abilities of people with disabilities. Recognizing the wide range of skills and education within the special needs workforce (and the company's need for such diverse talent), CVS Caremark offers two very different internship opportunities. In order to recruit pharmacists, it works with the American Association for the Advancement of Science (AAAS), which coordinates a summer internship program for science students with disabilities. "This past year, we interviewed eight kids who were good at math and science; pharmacy would be right up their alley," says CVS's Stephen Wing, Director of Workforce Initiatives. "They all had 3.9 or 4.0 grade points, and really refreshing attitudes. We offered five of them internships; we would have taken them all if we could have. One student who's blind is now working at NASA, helping to find a pathway for a manned mission to Mars. These are smart, sharp kids; we would have lost out if we hadn't considered them."

CVS Caremark also considers other groups of people with disabilities, offering programs and on-the-job training for people with cognitive disabilities. In its *New Vision* program, it teaches a short course in basic photography. People who successfully complete the program then move on to a regional learning center, where they're taught to handle the one-hour photo process. Finally, they complete an internship at a store. "Having taken the photography course, they know to ask things like, 'Do you need new batteries?'" says Stephen Wing. "They end up selling extra products, and are great at customer service. In addition, our other employees get to know them; they become part of the team."

⊃ **Positive Perspectives: Internships Prove Potential**

Several years ago, Todd, a student with autism, started a training program at a CVS/pharmacy in Cincinnati. CVS's Stephen M. Wing relates his story:

"When I met Todd, his parents took me aside, and said, 'He's not going to be able to run the register or anything. We just want him to get to work on time, get used to ▼

things like that.' When the trainer came in later, not knowing anyone, he pointed at a couple of people, including Todd, and said, 'You and you, come with me to the register.' During grand opening, Todd's parents walked in, looking for him. When they saw him running the register, they broke down—it was very emotional. Todd now has his own computer repair business. He still loves CVS/pharmacy, and we still admire him. You just can't stereotype people, or say, 'They can't do this, or they can't do that.' You have to give them a chance."

Speaking of Your Team . . .

Your employees may be your best recruiting tools: have you considered engaging them in your recruiting efforts? I bet not. Think about it. Your employees, who are already dedicated to your company, have sons, daughters, spouses, and friends with disabilities. Ask your employees to help you recruit.

Typically, when I first present this idea, most people stare at me for a minute, then nod and say, "That's cool." It *is* cool. What a wonderful way to bring someone into your company! It gets better. Your new employee with a disability now has a partner in the company. "Employee recruiters" want their friend or child or spouse to succeed, and will help them to become the invaluable employee you want and need.

An added benefit? You don't have to reinvent the wheel. You already have employees who can help you recruit. In fact, you probably already have an "employee referral program" in place. Use what you have. One caveat: you have to let your employees know that you're interested in hiring people with disabilities. They won't figure it out on their own. If they don't know you're interested, they're not going to send that great potential employee to you.

Great Grads

Many great employees come to companies straight from college. If your company recruits recent graduates, make sure your recruiters connect with departments, organizations, and colleges and universities that serve students with disabilities. Some higher learning institutions are dedicated to students with disabilities, like the venerable Gallaudet University, which has been serving students who are deaf or hard of hearing since 1864. Most mainstream colleges have a Disability Services Department, and many have outreach and specialized programs for students with learning or cognitive disabilities.

How to find these schools and organizations? "The co-leader of our disabilities network, Mike Gartner, works closely with P&G's recruiting team," says Ann Andreosatos, North America Region People with Disabilities Leader for Procter & Gamble. "He helps the team identify and work with external organizations that aid P&G with our disability recruiting efforts, and ensures that we have strong, effective relationships with these organizations in order to draw top talent."

Besides network building, Mike Gartner also helps recruiters to highlight the fact that Procter & Gamble is a disability-friendly company. Though they already provide the recruiters with information about disability etiquette, Procter & Gamble plans to develop an internal training program where recruiters will be certified in this special recruiting capability. Says Ms. Andreosatos, "A strong foundation in disability awareness and etiquette will ensure our recruiters are confident and engaged with our potential candidates."

The Right Stuff

Recruiters need to feel confident, and they need to have the right tools. My business card is in Braille: the front of the card is printed, the back is Brailled. Why do I do this? The percentage of people I meet who are blind is not huge (and many of those I do meet do not read Braille). That's not what's important. What's important is the message. I am branding myself as someone who cares about and is interested in people with disabilities. People think my business card is amazing, but it's no million-dollar idea. You too can do this. And you should, if you truly want to reach out to the disability community.

> ⤳ **Inspiration & Innovation:**
> **Leading Recruiters Down an Accessible Path**
>
> WalMart's Associate Resource Group LEAD (Leading and Empowering Associates with Disabilities) advises WalMart's recruiting team. The group not only ensures that recruiting material content is accessible, but also that the materials will appeal to potential associates with disabilities.

When reaching out to specific populations, it just makes sense to include them in your promotional materials. Do your recruiting brochures include photos of people with disabilities? Do you have those brochures available in accessible formats? Have you used appropriate language? If you're not sure, check out the tips in Chapter Three. Ensure that your materials include positive depictions of people with disabilities (no photos of empty wheelchairs, please), use disability-friendly language, and of course, are accessible to everyone.

Review your website. Is it accessible to people who are blind or have low vision? Many of them use a screen reader to access the web. Some websites don't "talk to" screen readers, leaving out big chunks of important information. If you have videos on your site, are they captioned? If not, you're missing out on the deaf and hard of hearing communities. As you can imagine, it's doubly important to ensure the accessibility of your site if your application processing is online. If your application isn't universally accessible, you need to provide an alternative format, and clearly indicate that option on your site. You'll find some web-accessibility resources in Chapter Six.

Don't Forget . . .

I realize that this chapter has focused on recruiting people with disabilities, but keep in mind the other two segments of the special needs workforce: older workers and parents of children with special needs. Though some organizations actively recruit these groups, more often, a company's success is a result of retaining these valuable employees by properly supporting them. You can provide that support by employing many of the techniques discussed later in this book: training, providing employee resources, developing work-life groups, and so on. You'll be able to dive into the potential of this workforce, knowing that your organization is ready to truly welcome them.

Organizational Readiness: R&R

I can almost hear you saying, "How does organizational readiness contribute to R&R?" My definition of R&R is slightly different than most. I think it means "Recruiting and Retention." "Right," you may say, "we've already talked about that." But I'd like to add one more thing: recruiting and retention is as much about organizational readiness as anything else. If you're not ready, you may find yourself with a revolving door. A colleague once told me that he'd been hired by a company that was extremely successful at recruiting people with disabilities—and equally proficient at losing them. He said, "The company seemed great when they were recruiting me, but once I was on board, it was a different company altogether." It may seem like an obvious disconnect, but it's not an unusual one. R&R is not just about having your recruiters say the right things; you've got to make sure that your company is prepared to *do* the right things to retain that employee. You've got to connect the dots. Then, if you've done it well—if the picture is complete—then, and only then, you can "rest and relax."

CHAPTER THREE
Different Strokes for Different Folks— Training

WHY does your company need disability-related training? Consider the following scenarios:

What should you do if you go to shake someone's hand, and discover that they have a prosthetic device, or no hand at all?

What do you say to a co-worker who tells you that her new baby was born with Down Syndrome?

What should you do if someone has a seizure at work?

Let's explore an even more complicated situation. Let's say that you have a co-worker who has been absent from work for six months. You heard that she was gone because she was undergoing treatment for cancer. One day, you get in the elevator, and see your co-worker—she's back, and has lost all of her hair. The rumors are most likely true. Not knowing what to say, you don't say anything, and get off the elevator. You feel terrible, and so does she—what a way to welcome and support your co-worker.

Cultural Competency

Wouldn't you like to know how to handle each of those situations in a positive manner? Training can teach you what to do in those situations before you run into them in real life.*

* Find positive resolutions for these situations at the end of this chapter.

Don't skip training because you think these types of issues may never arise. Remember the statistics mentioned earlier? The special needs workforce is bigger than the population of Canada. It's also a huge part of your workforce: remember that 15 percent of the employees who already work for you fit into this category. If you want your company to be culturally competent, to welcome and include the special needs workforce, training is incredibly important.

> ### ⊃ Surprising Statistics: Adult Bullying
>
> It seems that disability-related bullying extends beyond high school graduation and into the workplace. In its report, *Federal Employment of People with Disabilities*, the National Council on Disability noted that since 2002, harassment has been the most frequently alleged issue in disability discrimination complaints. Of complaints from people with mental disabilities, 38 percent were harassment-based. For people with physical disabilities, the number was nearly as high: 30.5 percent.

An equally important component of training is safety. Training can help people safely handle situations like the seizure incident mentioned earlier in the chapter. It can aid in terms of emergency preparedness, and even in feeling emotionally safe. By considering all access issues, learning disability etiquette, and creating a welcoming and inclusive environment, your company will also create a place where employees can feel safe discussing their situations.

And let's not forget the bottom line. All employees and prospective talent want to work for a company that is safe, culturally competent, and welcoming. By creating this environment (partially through training), you're on your way to becoming an employer of choice.

Let's add one more incentive: training in disability etiquette will enrich your business relationships, too. Take a page from Adecco's book. Like many other businesses, it has partners and clients with disabilities, including veteran-owned businesses. Its online training refers to these relationships, highlighting the importance of inclusion. The training offers benefits to both parties, making clients comfortable and helping Adecco to understand its clients' perspectives.

Please Do . . .

". . . make sure that seating is available at receptions, events, and the like. It's much nicer to have a small seating arrangement where I can sit with a few colleagues, than to have to ask for a chair and be the only one sitting in a crowd of people."

—Cindy Brown, co-author and ADA and Access Specialist, who lives with a mobility impairment.

Who to Train?

For some reason, there's always an assumption that training is intended for people with disabilities. That's not who it's for: they get it, they live it. That being said, be sure to include them, both for their perspectives and to give them a chance to learn something, too. I often get feedback from a person with a disability or a special needs parent who says, "Wow. I actually learned something in your training." Remember, there's diversity within disability. Don't assume that having a disability makes someone an expert in all aspects of disability awareness.

If training isn't for people with disabilities, who is it for? Some companies believe that training is only for front-line staff, or for people managers, or for Human Resources. Sure, all of the above people should be trained, but so should your employees who might have co-workers with disabilities, your recruiters who want to enlist top talent, and your executives who deal with business-to-business relationships. Here's my list of who should be trained, and why:

People managers

Most of these folks are wonderfully skilled at managing people; that's why they're in those positions. They do need to understand, though, that the needs and situations of employees with disabilities are often different from those of "typical" workers.

Front-line staff

Your receptionists, salespeople, security staff (and all others who deal with the public) provide customer service. These individuals directly and indirectly market your company to both customers and potential new hires. You need to know they're responding to every situation appropriately.

Recruiters

You want to recruit the best talent; that includes people with disabilities (visible and hidden), people who have friends and family with disabilities, and all others who value diversity. A well-intentioned but inappropriate remark from a recruiter can quite quickly end a relationship with a high-potential candidate.

Corporate executives

They don't need all the details, but they do need to know how to support their managers. More importantly, they set the stage that is your corporate culture.

Human Resources personnel

The buck stops here. If you're training your general employees and people managers, you'd better make sure you've trained your Human Resources folks, too. If an issue arises, your employees will go to Human Resources. If they haven't been trained, and don't know how to handle the situation appropriately, all of your hard work will go to waste.

Everyone else

You never know when someone is going to need this information. Prepare and empower your employees, both with and without disabilities.

Many of the successful corporations interviewed for this book—Ernst and Young, Starbucks, and WalMart among them—train (or are in the process of training) *all* of their employees. "In the firm, we cascade things starting at the top and work downward by rank or relevance," says Lori Golden, Ernst and Young's AccessAbilities™ Leader. "Within the year, our goal is have everyone in the firm undergo inclusiveness training."

⊃ **Positive Perspectives: Training from the Start**

"I believe that trainings should be integrated into the employee handbook, and that every new employee needs to have orientation that includes disability-related information."

—Shelley Kaplan, Director of the Southeast Disability and Business
Technical Assistance Center

Corporate culture plays a big role in training. Some companies believe in mandatory training for all. Some companies want trainings just for people managers, for customer service representatives or for recruiters, while other companies leave it entirely optional for everyone. Every company views training differently and knows what works best for its particular organization. Think about how your company views related topics and trainings; are they mandatory, or optional? Are they tied to personnel reviews? Though I believe in mandatory training for at least Human Resource professionals and people managers, at the end of the day, it will be up to you to decide what works best for you and your company.

Customize Trainings for Your Corporate Culture

Your corporate culture may also influence the manner in which you provide trainings. Some companies deliver training in person, while others prefer virtual delivery, though most combine the two approaches. Some roll disability-related training into other types of diversity or customer service trainings, whereas others provide stand-alone disability awareness and etiquette training. You know what will work best for your company, but before you get started, consider these two multi-faceted questions:

1. Who will provide your training?

I've found that most companies use one or more of the following:

- Professional trainers without disability experience
- Professionals in the disability field
- Employees with disabilities
- "Train the trainer" options
- A combination of the above

Let's consider the pros and cons of each.

Professional trainers without disability experience

These folks could be trained to provide the information you need—or think you need. If they haven't had experience with disability (either personally or professionally), they may not know some of the complexities of accessibility or the nuances regarding disability culture. They won't be able to offer the personal anecdotes that can be so important to these types of training. More crucial than that, since this is not their area of expertise, they may cut interactivity short, worrying that attendees might bring up unfamiliar issues.

Professionals in the disability field

Choosing these trainers makes sense. They generally have incredible expertise and will deliver the material in an appropriate, sensitive manner. They have the experience to deliver the information in a way that will resonate with the audience. They can encourage interactivity, and typically answer any questions that may arise during a training session.

Employees with disabilities

Yes, your employees who have disabilities or children with special needs will bring a lot to the table, but it's good to remember that there's a lot of diversity within disability. Someone who is blind may not understand the needs of someone who is deaf. If you do use folks from your own company, make sure to support them, and to see them as more than just your disability expert. "I think that people with disabilities in the work environment probably experience fatigue from being fairly isolated from others with disabilities, being teachers all the time, and being referred to as inspirational," says Deborah Dagit, Vice President and Chief Diversity Officer of Merck & Co. "Imagine if you were the only female in the division, and people asked, 'How would I do this for women? How can I find more women? Do women like it when someone uses this terminology?' I sometimes find it daunting to represent everyone with disabilities. We are such a diverse tribe with so many different needs and subcultures."

"Train the trainer" options

This may work well for your company, again depending on the type of training needed, and your corporate culture. Your newly-trained trainers may understand your culture well, and be able to relate to their peers. They may even have a disability or have a child or family member with a disability, but they probably won't have the level of expertise of the disability professional.

I do think it's important to have someone who has some personal experience with disability conducting your trainings. The disability community has a saying, "Nothing about us without us." It only makes sense; would you have a man lead training about women's issues? Shelley Kaplan, Director of the Southeast DBTAC, thinks it's a good idea, too. "When I co-train with someone who has an obvious disability, people pay attention. They realize, 'Hey, I could get in a car accident, too, this could be me or my spouse or my kid.' It becomes an 'aha! moment' when they take it personally."

Kevin Bradley, Director of Diversity Initiatives for McDonald's, illustrates one of these "aha! moments." "A few years ago, Karen Meyer, a local newscaster who is deaf, spoke to us regarding disability. She said, 'I'm a white Jewish woman. I'm not going to wake up tomorrow and understand your cultures. But all of you are just an act of God away from joining my club. Disability has no borders.' It really struck a chord."

2. How will you deliver the training or information?

Some companies roll disability-related information into other types of training. "We don't proactively train around disabilities as a topic unto itself. We have inclusiveness training which includes disability as a perspective," says Ernst and Young's Lori Golden. Other companies prefer specific disability-related training. Microsoft offers a "broad-brush" overview of disability etiquette, as well as "just-in time" training. "When we hire someone with an obvious disability, we offer awareness training tailored to the situation," says Loren Mikola, Disability Inclusion Program Manager for Microsoft.

Cisco Systems, Inc. uses both approaches: "We weave training into existing training programs, like our hiring and diversity trainings," says Marilyn Nagel, Cisco's Director of Inclusion and Diversity. "We also offer one-to-one coaching for any managers who request it, and provide training—both in person and through virtual webinars—that updates our employees with regards to new information and legislation, like the ADA Amendment."

Apples and Oranges

Cisco's method brings up another question: will you provide your training in person, virtually, or in some combination of the two? Different trainings have different requirements, and different employee groups require different information. You probably won't approach an Americans with Disabilities

Act training for your human resources managers in the same way that you'd deliver customer service training to front-line staff. Some training is definitely best when presented in an interactive role-playing format; other types of information might be fine when delivered via the web.

Virtual or online training can work well for large organizations, especially for those that are decentralized, for companies whose employees work many different shifts, and for techno-centric organizations. If you plan to deliver disability-related information on-line, consider the following elements of virtual training:

Interactive vs. Static

Websites, newsletters, and emails can be great way of communicating information and resources. Interactive training, though, trumps static information. People learn better when they participate. Use you website, but don't rely on it as your only form of training or communication; don't just "push out" information on a static website. Try adding a Q&A section, or provide a webinar.

Live vs. On-Demand

With a live webinar, everyone can listen, chat, and ask questions. It's probably the next best thing to an in-person training, though it may not offer the same level of comfort. It can be more difficult for both trainer and attendees to understand concepts and to feel "safe" sharing experiences, as neither can read the body language or facial expressions of those asking or answering questions. On-demand virtual trainings may not be as interactive, but they do allow employees to access the information when they need it.

Verbal vs. Visual

People learn differently. Adding visual components, such as photos and charts, to a presentation will help to engage different types of learners. Video can be especially helpful when discussing case studies or exploring possible scenarios. McDonald's, for example, teaches its employees how to best serve their customers with disabilities by showing video vignettes with typical customer interactions.

I believe that case study or scenario-type training is best presented in person, so that trainees can interact, ask questions, and come up with solutions by brainstorming with others. Actually, I believe that disability-related training in general is most effective when delivered in person, using real life examples, and providing an opportunity for trainees to bring their experiences to the table. I don't think that virtual training alone resonates in the same way. You're less likely to have that personal connection—that "aha! moment." If your company is not too decentralized and can afford it, in-person training is best.

When that scenario isn't possible, make sure that you're mindful of the different types of training and deliveries, and the people who need the training the most. People managers, human resource professionals, and recruiters are the folks who will most benefit from in-person training. They're the ones who are on the ground, who have to direct everyone else. They're the role models who illustrate best practices for the rest of your company. It's critical that they have experiential training that addresses their needs, and is relevant to their everyday work.

Experience—the Best Teacher?

Experience can be powerful. Many organizations use experiential training that simulates having a particular disability. Trainees might be blindfolded, or use earplugs, or walk with crutches. This type of training often has a great impact on those attending, as it did for CVS's Stephen M. Wing. "We had to go to work, and to use a wheelchair or crutches, from the moment we left home. It showed us how difficult it can be to get up ramps, or to maneuver around. That effort exposed the fact that people are people; they just have to figure out how to go through the challenges."

Many people without disabilities find this type of training very compelling. Some disability advocates, though, feel that these trainings give a false impression of disability. After all, even if you're using a wheelchair for the day, most of your co-workers, family and friends know that you're not disabled. You may experience the physical difficulties, but not the emotional and social ones. So, use these experiential types of trainings to help you understand some of the physical aspects of disability. Use disability-related experiential trainings, not in a classroom setting, but in your facilities. Navigate throughout your buildings, your outdoor spaces, and your parking garages, so that you can see whether any doors are especially heavy, which counters are too high, or where lighting is especially poor. The impact will be just as great, and you'll learn how to make your facilities—and your company—more disability-friendly.

Walgreens used to use the blindfolding, wheelchair-using type of experience. "Though it was eye-opening," says Deb Russell, Manager of Outreach and Employee Services for Walgreens, "we found that taking managers to a place where people with disabilities were employed was much more valuable. We now hold 'boot camp' in our South Carolina facility. Managers spend time on the floor, where they can see people with disabilities as productive, valuable members of the workforce. Our goal was for the managers to eventually forget that the employees had disabilities—and they did forget." The managers who went through Walgreens' "boot camp" also responded differently to "you be the judge" training scenarios. "Because they'd gotten over the novelty of disability, they recognized that they could often apply the same responses to situations, whether or not an employee had a disability," says Ms. Russell.

Please Don't . . .

". . . overcorrect. Once at a café, I went the counter to ask where the napkins were located. They gave me a bunch of napkins. When I sat down at my table, there were napkin holders, filled with napkins. People get so preoccupied with the disability that they get totally discombobulated."

—Loren Mikola, Microsoft's Disability Inclusion Program Manager, who is blind.

What Goes into Training? People, First

Walgreens is helping to teach its managers to think of people with disabilities as people first. That's huge; it's one of the deep-down truths that everyone needs to learn, and that should be included in your training. It's important enough, that I always begin and end my training sessions by saying, "People with disabilities are individuals with families, jobs, hobbies, likes and dislikes, problems and joys. While the disability is an integral part of who they are, it alone does not define them. Don't make them into disability heroes or victims. Treat them as individuals."

> ### Please Do . . .
>
> ". . . ask **me** what I want. Every once in a while, I'll be at a restaurant, and the server will ask my friend, "What does he (meaning me) want?"
>
> —Loren Mikola, Microsoft's Disability Inclusion Program Manager, who is blind.

By beginning your disability etiquette or awareness training with this idea, you let your trainees know that you are approaching the topic of disability from a "people first"/social justice perspective, which can help people to get comfortable and talking. Though some trainers start out by explaining the Americans with Disabilities Act, I believe that beginning the conversation with the law can make people feel rigid. Everyone doesn't need to know all of the legal requirements. They need to know what your company expects of them, which is that they will treat everyone—no matter their level, job function, or ability—with respect, as people first.

> ### Please Do . . .
>
> ". . . recognize me for my abilities, not my disabilities."
>
> —Dana Foote, KPMG's Audit Partner & Co-Chair, who lives with Multiple Sclerosis and cares for a sister with Down Syndrome.

My co-author Cindy Brown is also a trainer, and feels strongly about this issue, too. "If everyone truly considered people with disabilities as *people* first," she says, "they wouldn't make the well-meaning but inappropriate remarks, like 'Why are you on crutches?' or 'Can you walk?' Instead, they'd see people with disabilities as their customers, as their clients, as their friends *first*, and ask the same questions they would of those people."

The "people first" philosophy is best known as a language tool, and it's another important component of training. Put simply, the person comes before the disability. A "blind person" becomes "someone who is blind;" a "disabled person" becomes a "person with a disability." It's a simple idea, and it's always appropriate. You'll find this form of language used throughout this book. In fact, you may have wondered why I use the words "disability community" instead of "disabled community." Though a bit more complicated grammatically, it's for the same reason, to avoid labeling the community.

Not everyone cares about language, but a great many people do, and you should use and teach the language that the community, as a whole, recommends. "People first" language is your best tool. "Accessible" and "access" are also good terms. Avoid using outdated, negative, or cutesy terms, like "handicapped," "crippled," or "differently-abled." You may not imagine that your employees would use any of these terms, but my co-author, who has a mobility impairment, has heard all of them applied to her.

Please Don't . . .

". . . try to cure me. I know my body and my disability. Though I know you're well-intentioned, offering me the latest book, treatment, doctor, or even spiritual healing advice somehow implies that I'm not doing all I can."

—Cindy Brown, co-author and ADA and Access Specialist, who lives with a mobility impairment.

Speaking of Language . . .

You may remember that I coined the term "special needs workforce" to include three groups: older workers, people with disabilities, and parents of children with special needs. It's important to recognize those three groups as distinct from each other, with different needs and different language preferences. AARP's Dr. Percil Stanford confirms that "older workers" is the best terminology to use when discussing that segment of the special needs workforce. But why the distinction between "people with *disabilities*" and "children with *special needs?*"

The word "special" is not used within the disability community to refer to adults. People with disabilities do not want to be special; they want to be equal. They want to be people first.

The use of the term "special needs" is bit more complicated. Many, if not most, parents use this term to describe their children who have physical or mental impairments. Why? It's typically used by children's early intervention agencies and school systems, so there's a comfort level with that term. "Special needs" also engenders a sense of hope. Many parents provide therapies for their children with special needs in the hope they won't have those needs as adults.

Another reason: in my personal experience, I have noticed that parents often don't want their "typical" kids to play with those who have special needs. This not only isolates those children, but also their parents. A lot of social interaction takes place around school, play dates, and after-school sports-related activities. When a child is not able to participate in these mainstream activities, the parent doesn't have the opportunity to connect with the other parents, either.

I have found that referring to my children as "disabled" has made inclusion even more difficult.

For that reason, I, as a parent, use language (including "special needs") that minimizes my children's differences, hoping to promote inclusion.

An Essential Foundation

These kinds of nuances are precisely the reason why training is so important—how else would you learn this information? You need this information, and so do your employees. I believe that everyone in your organization, from top-level executives to facilities maintenance workers, *everyone* needs disability etiquette and awareness training.

Fear of saying or doing the wrong thing can keep people from saying or doing anything. "I remember the first time I went to a conference, using a wheelchair," says my co-author, Cindy Brown, who uses different mobility devices depending on her condition. "I'm really outgoing, and typically connect with a lot of people. Not this time. I was ready to leave by the second day. It was incredibly isolating." Ironically, Cindy had been invited to that conference specifically to share her perspective as someone with a disability. Disability awareness and etiquette training can help people to get over the fear that isolates the very people you want to include.

Please Do . . .

". . . offer help. For example, it isn't easy for me to stand in a moving vehicle like a subway. Don't feel that you're offending me by offering me a seat. If someone does get offended, realize that it's just that person. Don't let it stop you from offering help to other people with disabilities."

—Bonnie St. John, speaker, author, amputee, and Paralympic gold-medalist

---

Bricks and Mortar

Though I'd like to list all of the elements I think should be included in disability etiquette and awareness training, to do so would require another book. I do, however, want to give you a few guidelines about content.

"Person First" philosophy and language

Though we've already discussed this, I wanted to give you another reminder to include these ideas. They're that important.

Statistics

I often include statistics in my trainings. I think many people see the special needs workforce as much smaller than it is. Statistics help to reinforce the significance, potential, and power of this group. Shelley Kaplan of the Southeast DBTAC agrees. "I always start out with disability statistics and prevalence. It helps to break down whatever stereotypes people may have. They realize that people with disabilities are a broader group of people than they previously thought—and they could be one of them at any time."

A Few Basics

These etiquette reminders may sound like no-brainers, but people need to hear them (sometimes over and over again):

Know the road map to everything accessible. This includes not only things like ramps, but where to get assistive listening devices, and how to get materials Brailled, if necessary.

Treat adults like adults. No patting on the head—ever.

Don't assume anything about someone's cognitive state from their outward appearance. Think Stephen Hawking.

Be sensitive about physical contact. Avoid grabbing, patting, or touching.

Use "inside voices." For some reason, folks tend to talk to people with disabilities more loudly. If you speak softly, people who are hard of hearing may need you to speak up or speak more clearly, but for everyone else (including people who are deaf), it's most appropriate to speak in a normal tone of voice, just as you would to anyone.

Idiomatic expressions are okay. Don't worry about saying, "You should see the new James Bond movie!" or "Did you hear about Nadine?" People, even if they are blind or deaf, understand that those are just expressions—and they might just want to hear your review of that Bond movie.

Always respect the privacy of someone with a disability or someone who has a child or other dependent with special needs. Allow people to discuss their situation if and when they feel comfortable doing so. Above all, don't discuss their situation with others.

Please Don't . . .

". . . stare."

—Dana Foote, KPMG's Audit Partner & Co-Chair, who lives with Multiple Sclerosis and cares for a sister with Down Syndrome.

Some Specifics

Quickly review the basics above. You will notice that they not only apply to everyone with disabilities, they also apply to most people without disabilities. People need to hear that the rules of common courtesy apply to everyone. That said, there are other courtesies and ways of communicating that apply specifically to people with disabilities. Not only that, there are different considerations that apply to people with various disabilities. A good training will cover disability-specific etiquette. The list below is a very brief introduction to some of the information that should be included:

When welcoming:

People who use wheelchairs/have mobility impairments: Don't lean, push, or touch a person's wheelchair. It's considered personal space.

People who are blind or have low vision: Identify yourself and others when greeting, when in a meeting, and when leaving.

People who are deaf or hard of hearing: Recognize that there are a variety of ways to communicate. Ask the person what will work best, given the specific situation.

People with speech disabilities: Don't pretend to understand if you did not. Politely ask the individual to repeat the statement.

People who look different (facial differences, severe skin conditions): Don't treat them as invisible, but don't stare, either. Don't judge someone's ability by their appearance.

People with seizure disorders: I'd like to give you a bit more information here, because it's important (and because I promised I'd answer the questions at the beginning of the chapter).

- You can't stop a seizure; don't try.

- Don't try to mitigate a seizure by moving the person, or placing anything in his or her mouth (including food or water).

- Do try to prevent injury by moving chairs or other hard objects away from the person. You could also gently place a pillow under the head.

- Stay with the person until the seizure stops.

- Look for contact information or verification (most likely a bracelet or wallet card) that the individual has a seizure disorder.

Don't Stop There

There are many more categories I could (and do) include in training:

People of Short Stature

People with Difficulty Controlling their Muscles

People with Uncontrollable Vocalizations or Ticks/Gestures

People with Cognitive Disabilities

People with Respiratory Disabilities

People with Mental Illness

People with Hidden Disabilities

Don't forget to include this last category of people. These folks can have cognitive or physical disabilities that are not readily apparent. Don't judge, don't diagnose, and don't assume. By welcoming them with the basic tips above, you can help them to feel comfortable enough to ask for assistance, should they need it.

Finally, parents of children with special needs should also be recognized when providing disability etiquette and awareness training. Again, many of the basic tips will help them to feel comfortable and welcomed. Regardless of their child's disability, these parents, too, have hopes and dreams for their children, just like any other parent. A misplaced word or even negative body language could easily shatter those dreams. Let's say that your co-worker just told you that she's taking her daughter, who happens to have Down Syndrome, to her first piano music lesson. Having met the child and made assumptions about her abilities, you don't say anything, but your body language clearly says you don't think she'll be very successful. In the first place, you might be completely wrong about the child's abilities. In the second place, without saying a word you've sent that mother a negative message—a message that may be quite unsettling, may stay with her, and even cause her to rethink her own decision. Obviously, no harm was meant, but when something as subtle as body language can cause such potential harm, the importance of training becomes clear.

Beyond Awareness

I've given you a very few examples of the types of information that I believe should be included in a disability etiquette and awareness training.

Of course, there is a lot of other information regarding the special needs workforce. Consider the following additional training subjects:

Service Animals

Did you know that no certification is required for service animals? That animals besides dogs can be considered service animals? That they can perform a variety of functions, including alerting someone to an oncoming seizure? A training about these remarkable animals, the services they provide, and the rights guaranteed to people with disabilities who use them, is great for everyone, but especially helpful for any employees who deal with the public. It's typically a popular training, too, especially if it's facilitated or co-facilitated by someone who uses a service animal.

Emergency Preparedness

Everyone can benefit from this training, too, especially when disability-related issues are wrapped into general emergency prep or evacuation trainings. You might consider an additional, more detailed training for Human Resources and Risk Management departments, so that they can help to organize your emergency preparedness effort (more about this in Chapter Four).

The ADA

The American with Disabilities Act is many-faceted. There is much information (and therefore many trainings) your employees may need about this legislation, and the new ADA Amendment Act. For example, trainings dealing with Title I of the ADA (Employment), could include Interviewing, Testing, and Accommodations. I strongly suggest that ADA-related trainings be offered separately, to the people who need them. Human Resources professionals, legal personnel, and recruiters could obviously benefit from Title I trainings, while facilities folks might find trainings on physical accessibility helpful. Although they don't design your buildings, they are in charge of maintaining their accessibility.

Assistive Technology

These trainings can be a lot of fun, especially if your trainer can show off some of the newest technology. I'd advise offering these types of trainings to all your employees, maybe as a "lunch and learn." You never know who needs this information. Some employees may find it helpful for their child, their spouse, their parents, or even for themselves down the line.

Accessible Websites

Do you want everyone to be welcomed by your company and to understand all that you offer? Greet them with a website that's welcoming, inclusive, and accessible, and make sure that anyone who works on your site understands how to make it so. Trainings can alert your webmasters to potential (and typical) problems. It can teach them to avoid using information that's imbedded in graphics, to caption your videos, and to use "alt" tags so that screen readers can "read" graphics and photos. It can teach them how to marry "good" design with accessible design, so that everyone can access all of your information.

A Universal Welcome

By training your employees, your company will be equipped to truly welcome the special needs workforce (*and* the special needs market). In fact, I bet by just reading this chapter, you feel a little better informed. Remember those situations at the beginning of this chapter? You've already learned how to address one of them—"What should you do if someone has a seizure at work?" (Take a peek back at page 48 for the explanation.) Since you now understand "people first" philosophy, and have learned a few of the basic etiquette guidelines, you may have figured out the solutions to the rest of the hypothetical situations, too. Here's what I would recommend in each of those circumstances:

What should you do if you go to shake someone's hand and discover that they have a prosthetic, or no hand?

Typically, if the individual has a prosthetic/hook, shake it—it functions as that person's hand. If they have no hand, but a forearm is offered, shake that. If the person does not have a right hand/arm, shake the left. Most importantly, offer your hand, and follow the individual's lead.

What do you say to a co-worker who tells you that her new baby was born with Down Syndrome?

Let's talk about the "don'ts" first:

+ Don't talk with other people about the situation.

+ Don't ask the mother, "Did you have an amnio?" or, "Shouldn't you
  be home taking care of him?" You may not mean anything by it,
  but both questions smack of judgment.

To make a parent of a baby with special needs comfortable, treat the
father or mother as you would any other new parent. Ask to see a
photo. Put the person (and the baby) before the disability. If you have
a personal experience or relationship with someone who has Down
Syndrome (your child or sibling, perhaps), you might mention it, so
that your co-worker knows he or she can come to you for support or
resources.

How do you approach a co-worker who has cancer?

Welcome her back. It's that simple. Don't start with twenty questions: "Are you still having chemo?" or "What does the doctor say?"
Leave out the "I'm so sorry" pity factor. Again, put the person before
the disability. You don't need to talk about the cancer; you just need
to welcome your co-worker. A simple "It's great to see you," will let her
know she's been missed.

Training—Simply Irreplaceable

The above "solutions" are simple, but they're not instinctive. Think back
to the beginning of this chapter. How did you feel when faced with the
imaginary situations? What would you have done, before you had the
mini-training offered in this chapter?

Consider the "Please Do" and "Please Don't" advice scattered throughout this chapter. The situations mentioned reflect typical situations experienced by people with disabilities. Had you ever thought about them before
reading about them? I don't believe that anyone would handle all these

situations 100 percent correctly without some sort of training or personal experience. In fact, I would bet that the situations would be poorly handled (or ignored) more often than not.

> ### ⟳ **Positive Perspectives:** McLemonade
>
> When a crew member reacted poorly to a customer of short stature, McDonald's didn't just sit on its buns. It decided to bring all of the franchisees in that geographic area together for a training, and then expanded the training to include broader disability awareness. "We said, 'We're all in this together,'" says McDonald's Kevin Bradley. "If the person had made a right turn instead of a left turn, that would have been my restaurant. This is a learning opportunity."

All of that changes with training. People want to do the right thing: help them to know what that is. Train your employees (and yourself), so that you create a universally welcoming and inclusive environment. It makes everyone, disability or not, feel more comfortable. Comfortable employees are happier, more loyal, and more productive. Training is the best way to get there. That's the bottom line.

CHAPTER FOUR
Supporting the Swimmer — Accommodations

NOTHING. That's what it costs Adecco to accommodate one of its employees who is deaf-blind—nothing beyond the typical costs of running a payroll department.

Linda Katz, the employee's manager, was admittedly skeptical at first. "I thought, 'How's she going to do her job?' But we'd had a guy who was blind in our IT Department. He was phenomenal, he knew everything. He was the president of his baseball team—*his baseball team.*"

Linda's experience with her former co-worker helped open her eyes to the opportunity presented, and to the potential of her new employee. "She's a good learner, she's very pleasant, and she's as capable as anyone—no, she's more capable."

I bet you're still wondering how Adecco supported that "swimmer" at no cost. Like Linda, you may have made some assumptions about the employee. "I knew she was coming from the Helen Keller Institute, and I was focusing on the fact that she's blind," said Linda. She soon found that the employee has some sight, and is able to read. She does use a cane, and needed some assistance figuring out the building when she first started. A mobility instructor from the Helen Keller Institute, (the Adecco partner who had helped to place the employee) came to the office and worked with the employee and Linda. "I showed her how to get to the ladies room, and how to get out of the building in case there's a fire, that sort of thing," says Linda. "She also had a job coach, but after the second or third time, she didn't need her any more."

The job coach helped Linda and the employee with a few other accommodations, since the employee is also deaf. These accommodations ended up being simple, too. "We mostly communicate through Instant Messenger," says Linda. "Sometimes we write back and forth, too, just on a piece of paper."

That's it: large print, orientation to the building, instant messaging, and a piece of a paper and a pen. No extra costs for Adecco.

But is this no-cost scenario typical?

Having an employee who is deaf-blind is certainly unusual. The fact that the employee's accommodations cost nothing is not: **nearly half of all accommodations cost nothing.** In a 2006 survey conducted by the Job Accommodation Network (JAN), a service of the U.S. Department of Labor's Office of Disability Employment Policy, 46 percent of the employers surveyed reported that the accommodations needed by employees and job applicants with disabilities cost absolutely nothing. The typical one-time expenditure for accommodations that did have a cost was $500, but only $300 more than what was typically needed for an employee without a disability in the same position.

Surprised? If so, you're not alone. Many would-be employers cite the cost of accommodations as a barrier to employing people with disabilities. It seems that the true obstacle is a lack of education regarding accommodations.

This barrier, unfortunately, causes many well-intentioned companies to mishandle the issue of accommodations. They want to do the right thing, but don't know how to do it "the right way," or where to get assistance or information.

> ## ⇒ Surprising Statistics: Accommodation Benefits
>
> When the Job Accommodation Network (JAN) surveyed employers about making accommodations, they found the following:
>
> ### Accommodations are effective.
>
> Seventy-five percent of the respondents reported that the accommodations they implemented were either "very effective" or "extremely effective."
>
> ### Employers experience multiple direct and indirect benefits.
>
> The most frequently mentioned direct benefits were:
>
> - Retaining a valued employee (86 percent);
> - Increasing the employee's productivity (71 percent);
> - Eliminating the costs associated with training a new employee (56 percent).
>
> The most widely reported indirect benefits were:
>
> - Improving colleague interaction (67 percent);
> - Increasing overall company morale (58 percent); and
> - Increasing overall company productivity (56 percent).
>
> ### Accommodations produce financial benefits.
>
> According to the employers who participated in JAN's study, on average, for every dollar they put into making an accommodation, they "got back" a little over $10 in benefits.

The "Right Way"

And, yes, there is a legal obligation to do it "the right way." Briefly, under the Americans with Disabilities Act, employers with 15 or more employees must provide reasonable accommodations to people with disabilities who need them in order to participate in the application process, to perform the essential functions of a job, or to enjoy the equal benefits and privileges of employment that are available to individuals without disabilities. There are many great resources, like the nationwide DBTACs (Disability Business and Technical Assistance Centers) that can help you to understand what is required. That said, this chapter doesn't examine this subject from a legal perspective, but rather focuses on "the right way" that will help your employees and your business.

Make it easy

Can you imagine what it must take for someone to request a reasonable accommodation? First, employees have to self-identify as a person with a disability such as Multiple Sclerosis, and then ask their managers or HR generalist for assistance. No wonder so many people never request the assistance they need; no wonder they seem to have performance or management-oriented issues rather than disability-related concerns that can be addressed and accommodated. In order to make the process less onerous not only for employees with disabilities, but also for managers who receive requests, make sure that your process is easy to understand, and is well-publicized throughout your company.

Make sure it works

Sometimes, in an effort to make it easy, companies inadvertently create processes that actually make it more difficult for the employee. Here's a story I hear all too often: an employee comes to Human Resources (HR) with an accommodation request, and HR's response is to send the employee back to work it out with local management. If you're wondering what's wrong with this scenario, ask yourself why the employee skipped local management in the first place. Not only is there likely an issue that needs to be addressed, but there's an opportunity to train managers regarding best practices relative to handing accommodation requests. Think again about what it took for your employees to make the request in the first place. Don't smack them in the face. Don't send them back to local management without any other direction.

Don't make assumptions

You know what they say about the word "assume." For some reason, employers forget that it also applies to their employees with disabilities, and end up making an a—.... Well, you know the saying. Individuals with disabilities are just that, individuals. Even organizations that support people with disabilities and their families sometimes forget this. "All of our partner agencies said that all people with disabilities couldn't work overtime or flex, so we wrote exceptions to a lot of policies," says Deb Russell, Walgreens' Manager of Outreach and Employee Services. "We found out the first day (after opening our distribution center) that those assumptions were wrong. Once the Anderson workforce proved that we didn't need blanket exceptions to our policies for people with disabilities, we scrapped them. Now we say, let's wait and see if people can do this."

Involve the employee

What's the easiest way to avoid making assumptions? Involve the employees. They, best of all, understand their needs—and abilities. Adecco's Linda Katz says, "At first, I wasn't sure if I should give my new employee filing. Now, I leave it up to her. I don't make decisions for her. Instead I ask, 'Is this something you can handle?'"

Work with partners

Sometimes, though employees understand their abilities and limits, they may not know what accommodations will work for them. That's where partnerships become invaluable. Disability-related non-profits, assistive technology centers, and government resources like the Department of Labor's Office of Disability Employment Policy (ODEP) can all offer advice and assistance, helping both you and your employee to find the accommodation that best suits the situation at hand.

Create a disability-friendly corporate culture

Partners can also help to create inclusion and to foster an understanding of disability culture which, like corporate culture, can affect everyday work life. "The Helen Keller Institute taught our whole department a little about sign language. We had games, and got sign language cheat sheets," says Linda Katz. "We have a nice relationship with them." IBM creates a disability-friendly culture by making accommodations just another employment support. "We have a policy within IBM, a guideline called a corporate instruction that says that all employees will have access to all IBM technology available within the company, regardless of ability or disability," says John Evans of IBM's Human Ability and Accessibility Center. "Essentially, if you need something to do your job, we work to get it for you."

> ⮑ **Inspiration & Innovation:**
> **Accommodations "Outside the Box"**
>
> Speaking about a worker at Walgreens Anderson South Carolina Distribution Center:
>
> *"A young man who had ADHD and obsessive compulsive disorder . . . was focusing on the objects, and how he was placing them in the box . . . because of his disorder he was focusing on that and it was slowing him down. After examining the situation, the team down there, who's running as they go, came up with a chart that has a box for each number of boxes he's supposed to do an hour. He has channeled his compulsion over to this and now focuses on that. He now makes 150%."*
>
> —Randy Lewis, Senior Vice President, Walgreens

What is "It"?

Ahh, you may say, but my company isn't a "tech" company like IBM. No matter. Although the word "accommodations" conjures up visions of screen readers and voice–activated software, in reality, most accommodations aren't assistive technology, but changes in policies and procedures. Many employees don't need technology, they need breaks to administer their insulin, or a schedule that works with their transit needs. Shelley Kaplan, Director of the Southeast DBTAC, says, "Most accommodations really deal with flexibility." Flexibility, that's another one of those qualities that make companies an employer of choice—and it works for more than just people with disabilities. "I think flexibility draws people with all kinds of situations: disability, aging parents, individuals who have other interests in their lives," says Lori Golden, Ernst and Young's AccessAbilities Leader. "It's important not just when individual workers have disabilities, but when employees have family members with disabilities. That population is going to increase as baby boomers age and take care of aging parents."

Ms. Golden telecommutes, as do many of the people we interviewed, including Ann Andreosatos, North America Region People with Disabilities Leader for Procter & Gamble. "The ability to work remotely—whether sitting in home offices, working in the field to manage the business or even working somewhere around the world—frees up people to better manage their own personal situations. It's such an equalizer—and a great way to retain top talent and increase productivity," says Ms. Andreosatos. At IBM, it frees up a lot of people, with and without disabilities. "We've been using telecommuting at least 50 percent of the time since 1991," says John Evans, of IBM's Human Ability & Accessibility Center. "It's amazing that more companies don't do it. I think a lot of people think 'If I can't see them and touch them, they're not really working.'"

That's where the difficulties lie. "I knew of a great employee who had significant disabilities, as well as difficulties surrounding those disabilities. He had to take the bus, for example, and he'd wait for three or four buses until an accessible one came by. Then the lift would be broken or the driver didn't know how to operate it. His condition was also affected by heat and cold, and he spent a lot of time battling the elements, both natural and man-made," says the Southeast DBTAC's Ms. Kaplan.

A perfect candidate for telework, this employee did telecommute—for awhile. "It was working well until supervisors who were not part of the decision began to question why he was allowed to telework," says Ms.

Kaplan. "It actually got to the point where they were trying to deal with him from a medical point of view—trying to figure out why his body wasn't dealing with the cold—instead of working with him on reasonable accommodations." That's why it's so important to have comprehensive written telecommuting policies accompanied by established protocols for guiding the decision-making process. "It assures everyone that the telecommuting program is administered in a consistent manner, and minimizes misperceptions about the intent of the request," says Ms. Kaplan. "Most importantly, it enables an individual with significant disabilities to remain productively employed in his or her career of choice." It's not enough to allow employees to telework; expectations need to be made clear, and lines of communication kept open.

⮕ Surprising Statistics: The Truth about Telework

According to a study released by the National Science Foundation:

- 87% of the managers surveyed say that productivity either increases or remains the same while employees are teleworking.
- By not commuting, the average teleworker is off the road sixty-two hours a year, saving $1,201 a year in gas and other costs each.

And . . .

- Eighty-three out of 100 Best Companies to Work For (*Fortune* magazine 2009) offer some sort of telework.

Speaking of Communication . . .

Communication barriers affect many people with disabilities. People with visual impairments (as well as some people with cognitive or learning disabilities) often can't read typical print. People who are deaf or hard of hearing often can't hear conversations. Many of the accommodations needed for these folks are fairly low-tech. Order cards are just one of the accommodations devised by a Starbucks store for a barista who is deaf.

A customer points at a skinny vanilla latté on the card, and the barista fills the order. Simple. Walgreens, who employs many people with cognitive disabilities in their distribution centers, communicates in a variety of ways. "Communication needs to be visual as well as written, for people who can't read. We make sure that everything we do is effective in at least two out of three ways of communication," says Deb Russell, Manager of Outreach and Employee Services, for Walgreens. "For example, we have a sign for our evacuation rally point in our parking lot. The sign reads; 'Rally point,' but also has a picture of a group of people."

Communication isn't just an accommodation; however, it's an imperative when publicizing your accommodation process. If, as an employer you are covered by the ADA, you must post notices describing employment provisions of the ADA. It's also important that your employees know how to request an accommodation, and that you have a process in place. What type of process? Glad you asked.

RAC and Roll

In many instances, the process is left up to local managers. I hesitate to advise this; in too many cases, managers don't respond (or don't respond appropriately) to employees needing accommodations. Instead, I recommend developing and rolling out a Reasonable Accommodation Committee (RAC). Why?

To make it easy

When you have a RAC in place, an employee knows where to go to request an accommodation, and he knows his request will be reviewed by a committee that is educated about and committed to accommodating employees with disabilities. KPMG is in the process of creating such a committee. Barbara Wankoff, Director of Workplace Solutions for KPMG explains one of the reasons behind the decision: "We didn't want the process to become a bureaucratic obstacle. If someone wants a larger monitor or higher computer desk, they shouldn't have to go through layers of approval."

To make sure it works

Managers may make accommodation decisions based on their perception of how an accommodation will impact their budget. You can imagine that this could be intimidating, maybe even to the point where an employee doesn't make a request. Some of you may secretly be thinking, "Well, that's okay, we won't have the cost." You also won't have the productivity. And what if the request is a safety issue? If that employee gets hurt on the job, you can bet there will be a bigger cost. And lastly, remember what was said earlier about accommodation costs—or the lack thereof? RACS take the onus off individual managers. The committee makes sure that the process works, no matter who the manager, or where the worker is employed, while allowing a company to track costs, types of accommodations, and even geographic trends or issues.

To create a disability-friendly culture

One of the most important reasons to have a RAC is to show your employees that you have a process in place that is fair and equitable across the footprint of your organization. "A Reasonable Accommodation Committee will help us to make sure that we're consistently applying things, and giving the benefit of the doubt to people with disabilities in an office in Omaha Nebraska as well as a huge city office in New York," says Dana Foote, Audit Partner & Co-Chair of KPMG's Disability Network, who's in the process of assembling a RAC. "We want this RAC to help us track what requests have been made, and to be what you might call 'an appeals court' if people aren't getting the help they need locally."

To save you money

One of the first questions for Dana's disabilities network advisory board was, "How much are we spending on accommodations?" "We couldn't answer," she says. That's another reason that KPMG decided to organize a RAC. "Currently, employees raise a need and it does get addressed through HR, but to date we've had no way to track that or to share across locations," says KPMG's Barbara Wankoff. "People do a lot of research about what technology is available and how to implement something, but we haven't been able to leverage that across locations." A RAC will be able to give KPMG an idea of how much (or how little) it is spending on an annual basis. Since the requests are centralized, it will be able to coordinate research and streamline costs. A RAC may save you more than money. Having this committee won't keep you from getting sued, but if you do get a complaint, it does show that you have a formalized process in place.

If these points sound familiar, I'm emphasizing them because I believe that creating a RAC is part of doing things "the right way." If they don't sound familiar, you might want to reread pages 57–58.

➲ Accommodating and confidential

Shelley Kaplan, director of the Southeast DBTAC, reminds us that information about disability and reasonable accommodation should be kept confidential. "Not only that, but it should be kept in a file apart from the person's personnel file." One well-intentioned mistake: "We had an employer here who had a leave pool, where people could donate their leave to someone who needed it. People wanted to know who their leave was going to and why. You can't tell them that. They just need to know that it's going to someone in need."

How Does a RAC Roll?

Now that you understand the reasons for developing a Reasonable Accommodations Committee, let's move on to its function and organization. What, exactly does a RAC do? Obviously, it reviews requests for reasonable accommodations. Its members should be educated about what types of accommodations are available, where they can be purchased if need be, and what they might cost. All requests for accommodation pass through this group. The committee will evaluate the individual requests, and have the information needed to make good decisions. If technology or licenses are required, its members will know what's in place within your organization, and know the go-to people who can help research the accommodations. The committee will sign off on purchases, and over time, will be able to offer input regarding request patterns, costs, and even themes relative to geography. For example, in areas with severe winter weather that impedes mobility, there may be more telecommuting requests. And perhaps best of all, this group centralizes all of this work so that your company doesn't have to start the process over each time a request comes in. If the request is for a particular type of software, for example, they'll know if your company already has it, how to find it, and how to replace it if it's outdated.

This committee needs to be diverse. When considering the make-up of the RAC, think about all the possible accommodations that might be requested, then include people who represent all of these areas. A good mix might include key stakeholders from facilities, security, ergonomics, IT, communications, ADA/EEO, Diversity, HR, Work-Life, Learning and Development, even an Absence Management department, if you have one. Don't forget to include a stakeholder or two who represent the "business" side of your company (e.g., owners of specific products or services). Remember that accommodations are about improving the efficiency and productivity of your company. If you want your RAC to be taken seriously (and you do), also make sure that your committee members carry the authority and seniority that can make things happen.

Decide whether your RAC will be national or regional in scope, and include committee members from the various geographic regions represented. A few more questions to ask when organizing a RAC:

- How often should the committee meet?

- How long should members be on your RAC? Do you want term limits?

- When an accommodation request comes in, does the whole group need to meet? Maybe just a quorum?

- What's the process? However you answer this question, be detailed and thorough.

- How will your employees know about the RAC?

Once you have the RAC up and rolling, make sure that people know how to access it. Communication is key: not only for your employees at large, but especially for people managers who need to understand their role in the new reasonable accommodation process. Educate *all* of your employees: people with disabilities need to know how to make requests, and managers need to understand how to do it on behalf of an employee. Let me say this another way: no matter how incredible your program, or how dedicated your participants, the end result and success of a RAC hinges on communication. Every company communicates with its employees in a variety of ways. I have found that the intranet is an extremely useful tool, and recommend that all the policies and procedures around reasonable accommodations be available online.

The Budget Question

Money matters. That's why this chapter opened with a story of no-cost accommodations, and it may be why you choose to have a centralized accommodations budget. Like a RAC, a centralized budget can save you time (which is money), and can take the onus of decision-making off a manager's shoulders. By centralizing a budget, accommodation decisions are made on their own merit, not on how much is available in a certain budget. "Perception is reality," states Loren Mikola, Disability Inclusion Program Manager at Microsoft. "If existing employees perceive that a new employee is going to need a certain accommodation, and if that goes against the yearly budget for the team, they won't get new PCs for the year, or so they think. With a centralized budget, it's divorced from their team, and they don't have to worry about it. It's a good thing for new employees as well as the managers. It'll make managers more comfortable hiring someone with a disability, because now all they have to do is to ensure that the employee does his or her best work." Microsoft centralizes all its budgets that may touch on accommodations—adaptive technology, workspace accommodations, and even ergonomics. "We think it's the best way," says Loren. "It's even more so, in critical economic times, because this way the decision doesn't go against a team."

Difficult economic times are challenging for everyone, but perhaps even more so for workers requesting accommodations. An employee may fear that a request will have a negative impact, even thinking, "With all of the cost reductions, if I request an accommodation, I'll be the first to go." It may be obvious that accommodation decisions should never be based on the current economic situation, but as Loren noted, equally as important is the *perception* that requests are considered in a fair and equitable manner. By centralizing your reasonable accommodation funding (and taking it out of local managers' hands), you can help to counterbalance any fear that your employees may have.

To ensure that your centralized budget works as well as Microsoft's, look after the details when establishing the centralized fund. What are the sources of these funds? Who maintains their oversight and accountability? How is the opening balance determined? If additional monies are needed, what process determines the need and the amount to be added? The answers to these questions will be different for each company. A RAC can provide your company with an accommodations history, which can give you a good sense of the funds needed, and their distribution. The committee can help your company to predict the future in regard to accommodations (though the future holds no guarantees, of course). You don't have to have a RAC in order to have a centralized budget (Microsoft doesn't), but having one will help you to answer some of the above questions.

More Money Matters

Turnover costs money; costs incurred can run up to 150 percent of an experienced worker's annual salary. The Society for Human Resource Management's (SHRM) June 2006 Workplace Forecast Survey and Organizational Development Special Expertise Panel findings indicate that keeping key talent is one of the greatest concerns among employers. If you're one of those employers, consider this: accommodations help you keep those valued employees.

The Job Accommodation Network (JAN) answers a hotline for employers (a great free service, by the way). According to a survey, 83 percent of the employers who called for accommodation information did so to retain or promote a current employee. The employees they wanted to retain had been with them an average of seven years. The workers had average hourly wages of $13.70, or average annual salaries of about $47,000, and tended to be fairly well-educated: 53 percent had a college degree or higher.

Don't those sound like employees you want to keep? And did you notice that **83 percent** were making accommodations to *retain* workers? I emphasize this point, because I believe that most employers, when they think about accommodations, think about them in terms of new hires with disabilities. Of course, that's part of the equation, but it's good to understand that accommodations help greatly with retention, and that saves you money.

Accommodations can also make you money, by increasing productivity. As mentioned previously, accommodations increased individual productivity by 71 percent, and overall company productivity by 56 percent. Accommodations actually help your employees without disabilities, too.

Keeping Workers Productive (and Happy)

Kaiser Permanente has an interesting best practice that assists all of its employees, builds an inclusive culture, and ensures the effectiveness of its workforce. Recognizing that it's often difficult for employees with chronic conditions to disclose their disabilities or impairments, Kaiser Permanente inaugurated its Integrated Disability Management Program. "Before IDM, employees who had chronic conditions had to choose, 'Should I call in sick to work, because my arthritis is too bad to be handling patients today, or do I disclose that my healthcare provider has advised me to restrict these activities?' That's a horrible choice for employees to make, to fear that they may lose their job," says Robin Nagel of Kaiser Permanente's Integrated Disability Management Program (IDM). "Our new program will make it easier for employees to disclose medically managed chronic conditions which may result in disruption of their usual work capacity."

In the program, which Ms. Nagel calls "a work in progress," a unit-based team works with employees and managers to provide solutions that work for everyone. Ms. Nagel explains, "For example, if an employee's doctor had prescribed restriction from certain activities because of a flare-up (of a chronic condition), the IDM case manager might say, "Since your doctor wants you to avoid A, B, and C, I'm going to work with your manager to see how we can work with this restriction. If we can't, we'll assign you to temporary transitional work in another department, where you can be productive, and won't lose benefits or money."

This program also decreases "presenteeism" (being at work in a less-than-functional state), and works for those who might have temporary impairments. Mary E. Lewis, RN, had worked for Kaiser Permanente for eighteen years when she began to have mobility issues. "In 2006, I finally faced the fact that I could no longer perform my usual work. I needed both my knees replaced. . . . Without IDM I would have been off work for six months or longer. I did not have that much sick time built up to cover the extended leave. IDM allowed me to work between surgeries, and after the second one. Working brought me peace of mind, kept me financially solvent, helped my employer, and my ill time covered the time I medically had to be off work. . . . The knee replacements have allowed me to enjoy life again, have the physical and mental energy to work, and to the benefit of Kaiser Permanente, I am providing quality patient care once more."

Mary's not alone. Though she may not be considered a person with a disability, she needed some assistance. Many people, especially older adults, may find themselves in the same boat. The concept of disability or even workplace accommodations may be distressing, even to workers who could benefit from support. The solution? Go back to one of the key elements of accommodations: flexibility. "We have to start paying attention to the way we arrange schedules, or hours, or caregiving," says Dr. Percil Stanford, Senior Vice President and Chief Diversity Officer for AARP. "We've gotten so used to being carbon copies of each other, we don't think about adjustments. Not everyone is going to be doing things the same way."

Universal Design for Individuals

One of the principles of Universal Design is "equitable use;" design that works for many people with diverse abilities. This type of universality, in both policy and design, is as important as flexibility in retaining workers. "I would encourage us to look at our work environment as part of our lives. That environment should be friendly and supportive throughout *all* of our work lives," says Dr. Stanford. "Over time, I hope that this will be an everyday way of doing business."

For Starbucks, it already is an everyday part of business. "To us, universal access is designing a product or process or environment or communication in a way that's broader than the mythical average," says Marthalee Galeota, Starbucks Diversity Program Manager. "We think that if we keep that in mind, then when my over-fifty eyes need larger print and more lighting, I won't have to look for it, or ask for it. It will just naturally be there."

Universal access should be your ultimate goal—design that works for all people, all of the time. In the meantime, though, remember to make sure that your environment is accessible. Make sure, don't just assume (there's that word again). At Ernst and Young, Ability Champions (more on this group in Chapter Seven) conduct "wheel-throughs" of their facilities. Whatever improvements they note not only get addressed, but are included in construction standards, so that new facilities become even more accessible. "We go beyond ADA compliance," says Lori Golden of Ernst and Young. "For example, we not only look at space, building features and furniture, but we look at how the office is used. Where are the copiers placed, and can someone in a wheelchair easily reach them? We'll check out the day-to-day business process; where the supplies are located, how to access the visitor logs, etc. We'll go into the pantry and see where frequently used supplies—like coffee and tea—are placed. We'll identify the issues, and then, working with the office managers, make sure that things are easily reachable."

⤳ Inspiration & Innovation:
Taking Access to the World, One Building at a Time

IBM's real estate team uses a Global Building Accessibility Assessment Checklist. This tool measures the accessibility of new construction, determines the access needs of existing owned and leased facilities, and considers case by case situations.

Using this checklist, IBM has:

- Developed worldwide online training tools to assist the building assessment teams.
- Created a worldwide integrated building accessibility improvement process to proactively manage and accelerate improvements.
- Reviewed and modified all 272 high-priority buildings.
- Included barrier-free design in all new construction.
- Removed barriers from many existing facilities.

Prepare for All Possibilities

Nobody likes to think about disaster or emergencies, either, but we all need to consider the possibility, even more so since 9/11. We need to prepare, and to include people with disabilities in our preparations. Actually, we need to go beyond that. We need to consider the woman in her ninth month of pregnancy who works on the 40th floor. We need to consider the guy who went skiing and came back in a cast and on crutches. We need to consider the veteran with Post-Traumatic Stress Disorder who may have an unfortunate response to fire alarms, and the person with the cognitive disability who may not completely understand the situation. We don't want to leave any of them behind.

Know how to ask the right questions. "We don't ask 'Do you have a disability?' but, "Would you need help if there was an emergency?" says Ms. Golden of Ernst and Young. "This way, we include people who might be claustrophobic, people with smoke-induced asthma, and women in their last months of pregnancy. They all self-register, saying that they would need help."

Ernst and Young maintains this information in a database. I highly recommend that you do the same, ensuring confidentiality, of course. Consider, also, the nature of your employee's work. Since Ernst and Young has a highly mobile workforce, its employees' emergency information travels with them. "When people badge in to one of our buildings, if they're registered in the database, a flag will pop up saying they're at that location."

It's not only traveling employees you need to consider. What about visitors, or vendors? Do you include them in your emergency evacuation plans? Many companies have shared with me that due to the success of disability diversity initiatives, employees now feel comfortable bringing their children with special needs to Take Our Daughters and Sons To Work® Day programs. Remember these children, your vendors, and visitors when formulating an emergency plan. Make certain that *everyone* is informed regarding emergency evacuation information for people with disabilities.

"At our headquarters, we have emergency information at all of our emergency exits, and at the end of the hallways. We made sure that the information was accessible, and universally designed," says Crosby Cromwell, Manager of Disability Markets for WalMart. Universally designed communication is incredibly important in emergency planning; that's how you may reach some people with cognitive disabilities (not to mention people who don't speak English). Have the information in as many places as possible, even at your sign-in or security desk.

WalMart's corporate headquarters also uses a "buddy plan," another important component of emergency planning. "Buddies" are assigned to help people who require assistance in case of an emergency. It's a great plan, and used in many organizations. But what happens if someone's buddy is sick or on vacation that day? What happens if the employee who needs assistance is at a different facility, or in a meeting on another floor? You need to consider these questions. You might ensure that each person needing assistance has several buddies. You might try a database like Ernst and Young, or use technology that will enable people to evacuate more independently, like evacuation chairs.

You also need to practice. Yes, I know people hate this, but it's important for everyone. It not only makes all of your employees comfortable with the process, but it's also the best way for people to realize that they may need help. "When we'd conduct drills (at an Arizona State building), that's when people would realize, 'Wow, my knees are too bad to get down three flights of stairs. I guess I am going to need assistance,'" says my co-author Cindy Brown.

Assistance is one of the definitions of accommodations; that's why we called this chapter "Supporting the Swimmer." Flexibility can also be an important accommodation. Assistance and flexibility are both universal and individual—and they support more than just the swimmer. My co-author compares accommodations to her garden: "I can spray water all over my peas, but have to water my squash so that the leaves don't get wet. I have to support some of my tomatoes with cages, and I trellis my cucumbers, so that they don't shade the other vegetables. All of this work not only makes the individual plants more productive, but the garden, as a collective organism, is healthier, too." Isn't that really the bottom line?

CHAPTER FIVE
Everyday CPR —
Employee Benefits and Benefit Guidance

CPR PROVIDERS receive thorough training. People who incorrectly administer CPR could actually do harm to the very person they want to help. Believe it or not, it's the same with benefits. Without guidance, benefits can actually prove a liability, not just to the employee they're designed to assist, but even to the well-intentioned employer providing the benefits.

As you might imagine, benefits are even more important to the special needs workforce, and benefits guidance becomes more crucial for all concerned. Consider the following scenario:

Your company offers a great life insurance benefit to your employees. One of them, a father whose daughter has a disability, names her as one of his beneficiaries. When he dies unexpectedly, his daughter inherits a sum of money, enough that she loses eligibility for most government benefits, such as Social Security Income (SSI) and Medicaid (Medi-Cal (California)).

Social Security Income typically provides for housing and other community services, while Medicaid is in essence the government's health insurance. Whether she needs those services or not, she is no longer eligible. Federal legislation 42- U.S.C. 1382 (3)(B) says, "Generally, a person must have assets of less than $2,000 to qualify for SSI benefits and have personal income less than specified level." If the daughter's assets are reduced to $2,000, she can apply (or reapply) for benefits, but eligibility is not automatic.

This scenario is bad enough, but what if your employee's family decided to sue? Could they say, "Your company provided the life insurance benefit, but didn't tell us that our daughter would lose her benefits?" It's a huge question. There's no way to know the answer for sure, but the possibility exists, and it has happened.

The good news? There's a simple (and inexpensive) fix. I recommend that all companies, if at all possible, provide the appropriate guidance or disclosure. On every company form that includes a beneficiary designation, you should include a disclosure that states something to the effect of, "If the listed revocable, or revocable contingent beneficiary, is a person with a disability (child or adult), you may want to consult personal counsel. There is a chance that naming a person with a disability as beneficiary may result in a loss of government benefits." While there's no law that says you must make such recommended changes to your forms, why take the chance that one of your employee's beneficiaries could lose his or her government benefit eligibility? Without this simple piece of information regarding beneficiary designations, your employees, their beneficiaries, and your company could end up at a dead end.

The Benefits Maze

There's more to the maze. You've probably dealt with healthcare insurance issues at one time or another. Now imagine having to deal with those issues daily. Imagine calling your insurance carrier four times in one day, and receiving four different answers to the same question. I have found that, in many cases, insurance customer service agents do not have expertise in specific disability matters especially as they relate to the language in the plan. Their answers, therefore, are often inconsistent. Disability is not illness, and the management of disability can be very different from the treatment of medical illness. For example, many health insurance carriers offer speech therapy benefits. Historically, these benefits were designed to meet the needs of an elderly stroke survivor who needs short-term speech therapy. That's probably the information the call center or customer service representative will give your employee.

It doesn't matter that your employee called to inquire about his three-year-old son who has just been diagnosed with autism and will require speech therapy for an extended period of time. His son's need may not be a stated exclusion, and he may very well be covered, but it's tough working through the complex layers of information and communication that surround these issues. The customer service representative is certainly not an expert on autism and the employee is most likely not a medical insurance expert, and if his son is newly diagnosed, not an autism expert, either. The situation can become even more complex; some services are deemed educational in nature and not covered by the plan, while other services are medical in nature, and therefore covered. At the end of the day, the employee becomes frustrated, both with the carrier and with you as an employer, and yet still has no appropriate resolution.

There's another communication issue that often impacts employees' access to health care. I have found that the majority of declines that occur when using group health plans are not due to inferior plans. Instead, the letters of medical necessity that are submitted (by an employee's physician or other service provider) are not written appropriately according to the language of the healthcare plan. The medical issue may indeed be covered, if only the letter is worded differently.

Then there's the appeals process problem. People often misunderstand the process, and squander their limited amount of appeals. What a waste, and a frustration to all involved.

I'm not saying that you should change your health plans. I'm not telling you that you should deal with your employees' health issues. They don't want you to solve their issues. They want to be empowered with information about the plan, and more specifically, information as it relates to their unique issues. Help your employees understand how to use these benefits: isn't that what you created them for? I often hear complaints about low benefit utilization rates. Increase those use rates and assist your employees at the same time with a simple solution: education. Education leads to empowerment. Empowerment leads to satisfaction, and satisfaction leads to use.

Learn to Run the Maze

The right education is powerful. It can literally help your employees to receive the care they need. Let's say that Jane G. Employee needs physical therapy after an accident. Her healthcare plan states that she can have fifteen sessions a year. Jane would heal faster, feel better, and work more productively with more sessions. These sessions are actually available to her, if only she knew that her home health benefit offered an option for additional sessions. She doesn't know it, the person answering the carrier's toll-free number doesn't know it, but someone within the insurance company does know it. What's the solution? You can ask your health insurance provider to offer Health Insurance Empowerment seminars that include information about how to access critical benefits, optimally during open enrollment. Topics might include:

+ Therapies
+ Home health care
+ Durable medical equipment
+ Limitations and exclusions
+ The appeals process

Other types of insurance providers may offer seminars, as well. "Our life insurance provider offered a class to our employees where they introduced a specialized program/service that advises employees regarding special needs issues," says Barbara Wankoff, KPMG's director of Workplace Solutions. Most insurance carriers have people who understand the nuances of disability-related issues. Ask them to provide a class, a lunch and learn, or information you can use on your company intranet site.

Some companies have professionals within the firm who can provide assistance. "We have benefits advocates," says Lori Golden, AccessAbilities

Leader for Ernst and Young. "If you're having an issue with insurance coverage of a complex situation, maybe a chronic illness, or a need for durable medical equipment (either for you or a family member), and you're not getting the coverage you should, this is someone who will engage with the insurance company to troubleshoot for you."

Community partners may also be able to assist your employees. Many of the people Walgreens employs in its South Carolina distribution center have been receiving federally funded benefits and need to understand how their new employment benefits may impact them. "We make sure that they're aware of the benefit planning people in their community," says Deb Russell, Manager of Walgreens' Outreach and Employee Services. Its "90 Day" benefit education meetings are attended not only by employees, but also by benefits planning people within the community, who want to better understand what is offered. "One of the individuals came to the meetings three or four times. He wanted to feel comfortable about understanding our benefits so that he could explain them to our employees," says Ms. Russell.

Walgreens also offers follow-up meetings, which are opportunities for employees to bring someone, perhaps a family member, with them. These secondary meetings are comprised mostly of employees with disabilities. "We recognize that people who are coming from benefit systems related to their specific disability may need an opportunity to have more conversations about the interactions, and what they're eligible for," adds Ms. Russell. "We want to make sure that they realize that all benefits are available to all employees."

Walgreens also ensures that their Human Resources people have the information they need. "We don't train them to be benefits counselors," says Ms. Russell, "But we do educate them about the value of benefits counseling—how to help someone understand what they can get out of it, and where the resources are—so that they can whip out a brochure and say, 'Here's a number you can call.'"

Human Resources personnel can certainly help educate employees about their benefits, as can Employee Assistance Providers (EAPs). Don't put all your eggs in these baskets, though. I've consulted with many companies who assume that their EAP can provide all of the necessary information and education. Often it's these very Employee Assistance Providers who call me regarding disability-related issues. It's best to remember that many EAPs don't consider themselves experts in the disability field, and there are limits to what they can offer. Make sure that your company somehow provides the information and education your employees need.

More Ways to Get Through the Maze

If education is the map that leads employees through the benefits maze, then communication is the signpost that guides your employees and your company through the intricacies of that maze. Communication has to exist at every level of the benefit process. Let's say that your company offers on-site or backup daycare to your employees, or maybe even both. Do you know if it includes care for children with special needs? If so, under what circumstances? If not, why not? Find out—that's the first level of communication. The second level: if they don't offer daycare for children with special needs, ask them why. Challenge your vendors to provide your company with the services your employees so desperately need. Once these services are in place, make sure your employees are aware of them, and know how they can be accessed. Communication on all levels conveys to your employees that you not only understand their unique needs, but care enough to provide solutions to those needs.

The Benefits from Benefits

And lest you think that all of this education is just for your employees, let's look at the business case. What can benefit guidance do for your company?

Engage your employees

Employee engagement is a not only a corporate buzzword (okay, two words), but also a business imperative. When employees feel emotionally connected to their organizations, they put greater effort and pride into their work. According to a recent Gallup study, only 29 percent of U.S. employees are engaged: 54 percent of employees in the United States are not engaged, and 17 percent are disengaged. There are dollar signs behind these statistics. Highly engaged employees outperform their disengaged colleagues by 20 to 28 percent according to the Conference Board (2006), while low productivity by disengaged workers was found to cost between $243 billion to $270 billion, according to a 2003 Gallup poll.

Good benefits obviously help to engage employees: an even better tool is benefit education. Now employees know how to get what they need, and that empowering information came from *your* company. "Our employees did not know a lot about these areas, and they're really appreciative of any ways we help support them," says KPMG's Barbara Wankoff. "People have a general overview of what's covered, but when you get into a lot of the nuances it gets very time-consuming. We're not just providing a service to our employees; we're also saving them time."

Reduce absenteeism

Absentee management is such a big issue that entire conferences are devoted to it. By saving their employees time, KPMG just might be saving them absentee days as well. Employees who are well-educated about their benefits won't need an entire day off work to deal with the insurance company (this is not an unlikely scenario). Newly disabled or injured employees might be able to come back to work sooner, if they are able to use all of their benefits (as Jane G. Employee did with her physical therapy). A mother who has a child with special needs won't have to take time off work to find the daycare or medical information she needs. Her mind will be on her work, now that she doesn't have to worry about making myriad phone calls to the insurance company, reducing "presenteeism" for your company.

Become an employer of choice

When job seekers are interviewed about the reasons behind their employer choices, benefits rank high: for most people, it's not the dollars, but the benefits. Benefit education can also help to retain valued employees, who understand that without the information and support offered by your company, dealing with insurance issues could feel like a full-time job.

Protect your employee and your company

As we noted at the beginning of this chapter, without the proper benefit guidance, your benefits package could actually become a detriment.

Empower your employees

Educated employees are empowered employees. They'll understand what questions to ask, and how to ask them. They'll understand how to talk to their doctors so that their letters of medical necessity are worded properly. They'll know not to label a phone call an "appeal" if they haven't offered new information. They'll know the specific ins and outs of your plan as it relates to them—and they'll owe all of this to *your* company, who cared enough to support and educate them.

CHAPTER SIX

Gather the Gear — Employee Resources

EVER THOUGHT about getting a service animal? Exploring adaptive recreation opportunities for your kids? Or what to do if your condo association won't let you put a ramp to your front door? If you did, would you know how to find this information? Employees in the special needs workforce have to deal with questions like these on a daily basis. Many people have discovered some of the answers, only to have new questions crop up as their children mature, their disabilities progress, or their life situations change. New questions, new issues, new situations—dealing with those can seem like a full-time job. Employees often take vacation days, or use up weekend after weekend trying to find the resources and information they need. It can affect not only their off-time, but their choice of employer. How?

If you want to be an employer of choice, you have to understand and value the needs of your employees. Companies today realize they have to do more than just get their employees from meeting to meeting; that's why they have diversity and work-life departments, employee resource or affinity groups, and more. Remember, the talented employees you want to recruit have their choice of employer. If they have the choice of ten different employers, all basically offering the same salaries and benefits, what will make them choose your company? One way to distinguish your company from the rest is to show potential employees that you value them as individuals. How do you demonstrate this value? By giving them resources that help to support their individual and collective needs. It's also one of the keys to supporting and retaining the high quality people you already employ.

Gather the Gear at Your Fingertips

I'm sure you'd like to be able to provide one-on-one, in-person support for every employee who needs it. Between limited resources and an often decentralized workforce, that's generally not possible. You can support them, though, with a tool already at your disposal: your intranet site. Obviously, your company's intranet site supports your employees by providing them with information and links to resources within your company and within the community, but it can do more. People's needs (and this is especially true of people with disabilities) change from day to day. At any point in time, someone can have a need for this critical information. Your intranet site can supply needed information and resources in a just-in-time framework. It also allows employees to access all of this great information your company is supplying (more on that soon), *without identifying who they are or why they need this information.*

Someone may have just given birth to a baby with Down Syndrome, and desperately needs to find a Down Syndrome parent support group. Anyone can go grocery shopping and get hit by a car on the way to the store, resulting in a spinal cord injury and the use of a wheelchair. Anyone can lose a spouse and spiral into a bout of depression. I'm sure you realize that these scenarios characterize any number of your employees at any given time. It's these employees who need those just-in-time resources.

A 24-Hour, Serve-Yourself Smorgasbord

This self-serve information should be a veritable smorgasbord of information and resources. Here's a taste of some topics that could prove important to your employees in the special needs workforce:

Important Terms and Disability-related Language

Explain acronyms like ADAAG (Americans with Disabilities Act Accessibility Guidelines), enlighten people regarding person-first language (feel free to use the examples mentioned in Chapter Three), or clarify terms like "disability" and "special needs" when describing someone.

Disability Etiquette and Awareness

Help everyone to feel comfortable by providing etiquette tips, like:

+ When speaking to people who are hard of hearing, face them so that they may see your lips and facial expressions.

+ Never move someone's cane without permission.

+ Never push someone's wheelchair without asking.

(More tips in Chapter Three)

Government Benefits and Services

People often don't know what services are available to them (Can I receive orientation and mobility training if I'm losing my sight?), the criteria used to obtain the services (Can my adult child receive medical benefits if he or she is under my care?), or what rights they're granted (Does my son who has Cerebral Palsy have a right to participate in a "typical" summer camp?). Link them to the answers they need, and empower them.

Financial Issues

As explained in Chapter Five, listing a beneficiary on a group life insurance policy might cause a child with special needs to lose government benefit eligibility. Disability-related issues often intersect with financial ones, and often in ways you might not expect. Offer information on benefits guidance, government benefits and assistance, and planning for the future (more on this in the next chapter).

Educational Issues

Don't forget to include information about education. Parents of school-age children with special needs will benefit from information about laws that govern eligibility for and access to educational programs. Adults with disabilities (and parents of recent or soon-to-be grads) can learn about colleges and universities with programs and services for students with disabilities.

Support and Disability- and Disease-Specific Groups

Groups range from disability-specific groups, like the Hearing Loss Association of America to interest-driven groups like Blind Sailing International.

Advocacy Groups and Agencies

These organizations provide support and information about research, inform the community about events, and help people find the disability-related assistance they need.

Government Information and Resources

From the ADA to assistive technology, from FMLA to Fair Housing (yes, it covers people with disabilities), help your employees get informed by linking them to resources.

More

Add links to disability-related recreation and travel sites, to peer mentoring groups or parent matching organizations, and to accessible arts and culture programs. How to know what to add? Ask your employees, or better yet, your disability-related affinity group.

And last but not least, company-specific, disability-related information

Obviously, your company is going to want to tailor your site and the information included, to brand it with your corporate culture.

Cisco's site, for example, includes calendars of events, information about its work-life group, assistive technology requests, links to training, its mission statement, disability awareness education, videos, information about common disabilities and challenges, and even a section on famous people with disabilities. "We've included people like Albert Einstein and Magic Johnson, so that people can have role models in different fields," says Marilyn Nagel, Director of Inclusion and Diversity for Cisco Systems, Inc.

⊃**Positive Perspectives:** Albert & Magic

Albert Einstein is widely considered to have had a learning disability. He did not speak until he was three years old, and always had difficulty expressing himself in writing. Like Einstein, Magic Johnson has a learning disability. In addition, he lives with HIV, which is considered a disability.

Procter & Gamble is building an intranet site that will serve as a virtual resource center. The site will provide internal and external disability-related information, will support caregivers and will showcase Disability Champions: senior leaders who are sponsors, leaders of the People with Disabilities Affinity Network, and employees that simply create an environment where those who deal with disabilities can thrive. Ann Andreosatos, North America Region People with Disabilities Leader for Procter & Gamble, believes that the website will serve to further advance the culture of diversity at Procter and Gamble, giving particular support to the company's People with Disabilities Affinity Network. "We'll have monthly communications that will draw people to the website and create energy around enhancing our culture of diversity," she says. "We'll considerably improve visibility and engage a broader network—whether employees need support, a resource, or just a friend who understands."

Procter and Gamble has designed the virtual resource around need. It created a test group for its website, making sure to include a variety of employees: people who use wheelchairs, employees who are visually impaired, others who are deaf or hearing impaired, managers of employees with disabilities, HR generalists, and caregivers of disabled dependents. A young manager who is deaf and a finance director who has a special needs daughter co-lead the network, which also includes several parents of children with special needs. All of these people provide the information and the perspectives needed, and help ensure that the website is accessible to all.

Inspiration & Innovation: Accessible Websites

Ensuring accessibility to your website may seem like a no-brainer, but there are enough inaccessible websites out there to prove that it's not. Non-captioned videos, a lack of "alt" tags and poor contrast between text and backgrounds are just a few common issues. Get tips from the Web Accessibility Initiative (WAI) (www.w3.org/WAI), a respected, globally reaching, non-profit organization that develops:

- Guidelines which are widely regarded as the international standard for web accessibility
- Support materials to help understand and implement web accessibility
- Resources, developed through international collaboration

Get help from your employees, your partners, or your community. Ask someone who uses a screen reader or other assistive technology, or use your affinity group to review your site.

You may not have the wherewithal to create a disability-related subsite right now. No matter; you can connect the dots you already have. For example, if your intranet site has a web page about college education, include a link that leads to disability-related information, e.g., "If your child is a student with disabilities, click here." The link could lead to a database of colleges and universities with dedicated programs for students with disabilities, supplied by a trusted outside resource (there are some lists in the appendix to get you started). It's just one more way to provide information and resources, and it's especially inclusive; the information is there for all to see.

Let's Do Lunch

"Lunch and Learns" are a great resource tool: everyone can use some helpful information along with their sandwiches. That's the key: *everyone*. When marketing your programs, communicate to everyone. Don't just target disability-related groups. You don't want one group wondering why they've been segmented, and more importantly, you want the information to be available to all. There may be audience members with hidden disabilities, or who have children or family members with disabilities. You never know who can benefit from what information.

So what goes well with sandwiches: what types of information might you offer? If you have an affinity group, ask them—they'll have good ideas and possibly resources or presenters for you to consider. Presentations should reflect the diversity among disability, don't just stick to information that applies only to wheelchair-users, or just to adults with disabilities. Remember to include topics that are pertinent to families with kids with special needs, to vets with disabilities, and to people who may have hidden disabilities. This last group is often overlooked; make sure to include information about mental health issues, learning disabilities, and other cognitive or hidden disabilities. People with hidden disabilities comprise the largest number of people with disabilities, but whether it's due to stigma, or the fact that the disabilities themselves are often hidden, it's sometimes difficult for people to find the information they need. Another caveat: try to ensure that people with disabilities (and parents of children with special needs) are included either as presenters or panelists. As mentioned earlier, there's a popular saying in the disability community that should be your mantra: "Nothing about us without us." It's also a good idea to provide information that will be universally beneficial; presentations about benefits, or about planning for the future, for example.

Newsletters are another great resource tool. They can be topical, providing information about the latest changes in Medicaid, or they can be more general, e.g., covering a variety of community-wide events in celebration of Disability Awareness Month. I encourage you to include disability-related information in whatever newsletters you already have, remembering that you want to reach (and show support for) the broadest population possible. Include disability information in general articles about benefits or education, for example, and stories that deal specifically with certain disabilities or disease research. I recommend that your newsletter be electronic if possible. Not only is it more accessible (people who use screen-readers or need print magnified can use it easily), but you can engage your employees by encouraging them to comment, or share their personal experiences by writing articles for the newsletters. Articles can illustrate success stories, and feature employees with disabilities or parents of children with special needs (making sure to get their permission, of course). It helps to give a face to disability, and can be one of the best ways to create the inclusive, disability-friendly corporate culture that should be your goal.

More Gear to Get You to Your Goal

Not only do you want people to be aware of disability within your company (and within our world) but also to be aware of the incredibly important resources that you offer. Well-publicized intranet sites, events, and newsletters should be the backbone of your approach, but don't stop there. Consider email news blasts, or printed materials, too. Kaiser Permanente publishes an informative brochure that lists ADA-related information, tips regarding etiquette, FAQs, additional training tools for healthcare providers, and numbers to call to arrange for alternative formats. Ernst and Young has a similar brochure, full of flip sheets and quick guides on different topics (tips for inclusive conference calls, for using video relay, etc.). Both Ernst and Young and Kaiser Permanente also use small, easily-carried materials.

"We've found that the best way to teach people is to engage them with something that is a little different, brief and to the point, that's also portable and can be used in many different contexts," says Lori Golden, Ernst and Young's AccessAbilities Leader. Videos and posters featuring their own employees are also effective. They're currently working to ensure people with disabilities are included in other company materials. States Ms. Golden, "We're lobbying very hard to include them in the same fashion as we include people in different ethnic groups. If there are just two people in a (photo) shot, it may not be necessary, but if there are many, it's just realistic to include a person with a disability."

WalMart also includes its associates with disabilities in its internal (and external) communications, and it communicates in a variety of ways. "We have an intranet, *WalMart Daily News*, and WalMart TV, which is filmed at the home office, but broadcast throughout all of our stores and clubs," says Crosby Cromwell, Manager of Disability Markets for WalMart. "There are a lot of outlets for the disability story to be told."

Inspiration & Innovation: Employee Resource *and* Marketing Tool

Microsoft's new Inclusive Innovation Showroom uses real-world scenarios to illustrate how people of all abilities—including those with vision, mobility, and learning disabilities—can use accessible and assistive technology to customize their computing experience. The showroom, located on Microsoft's Redmond campus and open to both employees and visitors, uses four fictitious case studies that demonstrate how people with various disabilities can access their computers. A fifth case study showcases retired baby boomer "Ann," who uses a large plasma screen, and Windows features like High DPI, mouse settings, and custom color schemes in order to better see the text on her computer screen.

IBM's Human Ability and Accessibility Center (www-03.ibm.com/able/index.html) is a fantastic online resource for everyone. Users can check out case studies, web guidelines, information about laws, accessible technology, and of course, IBM's accessible products and services.

A Moving Story

There's an oft-forgotten chapter in the disability story. People with disabilities and their families have to plan much more than do "typical" adults.

What do I mean? Consider a typical family vacation. Your family probably decides on a destination, then figures out how to get there (plane, train or automobile), where to stay, and what you want to do. Now add "access'" into every step. Is the train accessible? The taxi to the hotel? The hotel? The attractions you want to visit? Is there medical care nearby, in case there's an issue? Now, of course, I'm not asking you to help plan your employees' vacation,* but I am asking you to take that scenario, and multiply it times ten. That's what happens when an employee with a disability, or who has a family member with a disability, has to relocate. And that's when they'll need your support.

> *You should however, take into consideration these difficulties when inviting employees with disabilities and/or their families with special needs to out-of-town conferences and special events.

Relocation issues are so time consuming and impact so many areas of their lives that some employees, not wanting to deal with the risks involved, may turn down the relocation offer, even if it's a promotion. "I don't think any company is completely prepared for all of the special needs associated with a move," says Deborah Dagit, Vice President and Chief Diversity Officer for Merck and Co. "For example, a lot of us can't utilize run-of the-mill healthcare." Fortunately Deb had worked with a national organization that advocated on behalf of people with her condition, so she knew that Johns Hopkins, about a three-hour drive from her new home, was a center of excellence. Even then, she had to make arrangements, transfer records, and connect providers in her community with the experts at Johns Hopkins. "I don't think the average citizen would know how to do it," says Deb. "And even for me, it was daunting."

There may be more than one family member who needs extra preparations, too. Deb, her husband, and their adopted children all have disabilities. "Being involved and engaged parents of children with disabilities requires a lot of time and effort with school systems as well as healthcare systems. We decided that my husband would work as a substitute teacher so that he could advocate in the educational system from the inside. I have a lot of experience in the healthcare sector, and know more about these systems than the average person would. Even with this unique arrangement, one that might not be possible to achieve in many families, we both feel like we both have more than full-time jobs."

And that's not even dealing with accommodations or work-related issues—some of which may not be obvious until the employee is actually at the new work location. "Some of the facilities here at Merck are on really big campuses, and are widely distributed around the world, so there's a lot of travel required. I had to figure out a strategy that would work for me to meet the demands of the job and minimize risk and fatigue," said Deb, who is also of short stature. She laughs about another issue:

"While we were closing on our new home, they put us up in a transitional living unit for the first three months that had been custom-built for a couple who were exceptionally tall. We had to use stepstools for absolutely everything!"

Paving the Way

Perhaps you're beginning to understand why an employee might turn down a relocation offer, even a great one. You can help. Make sure that assistive technology is ready and waiting for employees when they arrive. Help your employees to find the healthcare and educational resources they need. Ask what they need, and listen. "There are so many types of disabilities, and everyone has his own way of dealing with things. The best things you can provide are on-going receptivity to talking through questions that come up, and accommodations, like customized office chairs, disabled parking, and flexible work arrangements," says Deb. "The level of self-advocacy required is really high. It takes tenacity, patience, and courage."

I agree with Deb. When I moved out to New Jersey with my husband and two girls, I was lucky to work for a company that gave me the time I needed to get things set up—to interview a nurse, line up transportation, get a disabled parking placard, and so forth. I was fortunate, not only because I worked for a company that understood and supported my needs, but because I knew how to advocate, and how to find the resources that my family needed.

If knowledge is power, you can give your employees the strength, and maybe even the courage, that they need. Empower them, support them. As you can see, it's not difficult. You don't have to know it all. You just need to provide access to the resources your employees need. Show the world that you understand and value the needs of your employees, and you're well on your way to being an employer of choice.

CHAPTER SEVEN
Staying Afloat— Work-Life and Support

Balancing work and life in today's fast-paced world can be tough. Trying to do the best for you, your family, and your employer takes a lot of energy and planning. For people in the special needs workforce, it can be even harder to achieve that balance. My co-author, Cindy Brown, and I recently attended a conference together. We decided to go out to dinner with a group of colleagues at a nearby restaurant, just a short bus ride away. Because Cindy was using a scooter, it took us more than an additional hour to get to and from the restaurant. Nothing was broken or malfunctioning; it was just a matter of waiting for accessible transportation. That's an everyday occurrence for many people in the special needs workforce. They have to weigh issues and ask themselves questions that the rest of us may not consider: How long will it take me to get where I need to go? How many transfers are involved? What about child care? How difficult will it be to take my medications, service animal, or assistive device with me? How far will I be from home in case there's an emergency?

When my daughters were young, they both required nursing care due to their disabilities. My job at the time required a ninety-minute commute each way. If I didn't leave my office by 5:10, I'd miss my train home. I couldn't ask a neighbor to watch my girls, and nurses charge hefty hourly fees. I couldn't stay late for a meeting or a phone call. I had to be out that door by 5:10. Luckily my supervisor understood my situation, and worked around my schedule.

⮕ Surprising Statistics: Work-Life Balance for Special Needs Parents

According to a study by the Sloane Work and Family Research Network, 14 percent of parents of children with special needs require an additional 10 hours per week to coordinate their child's care. One-quarter of all special needs parents have been fired at least once, and cite their child's exceptional childcare needs as the reason for their termination.

At another conference, I met a gentleman who has a significant physical disability, but requires very little in terms of accommodation. He travels a lot for work but requires a little extra time on both ends to prepare and recover. He said to me, "Now, we could view that as an accommodation, as something I need to do my job effectively. For me, though, it's a balance issue. If I don't get that extra time, I become physically exhausted, which could result in an accident. Or I could come home to my family and be absolutely wiped out both mentally and physically. I'd be no good to them—or to my company the next day."

You want your employees to be on top of their game when they're at work. "Presenteesim" not only affects the productivity and creativity of one employee, it can bring down his or her team or department. Want another business-related reason to support work–life balance? Remember the Society for Human Resource Managers' study mentioned in Chapter One? That particular study revealed that work-life balance is the second most important societal trend. By supporting this balance, you'll have happier, healthier, more productive employees, *and* you'll position yourself as an employer of choice.

⮕ Positive Perspectives: Enabling Success

"I'm lucky to work in a very progressive organization that looks at everyone's full talents. We invest a lot in our people, so we want to bring out their absolute best. It just makes sense to do whatever we can to unleash the full potential of every one of our people."

—Lori Golden, AccessAbilities Leader, Ernst & Young

But what exactly does work-life encompass, and how can my company support it? Let's start with one of the more obvious supports: disability-related affinity groups.

A Supportive Group, not a Support Group

I sometimes hear companies say, "We don't support 'support groups.'" That's right; you shouldn't. You should be taking care of business. Affinity groups, also called "employee networks" or "employee resource groups," are not support groups. The goals of an affinity group are to bring employees with similar needs, interests or affiliations together, to help them become more productive, innovative employees, and to help their company reach its goals and objectives relative to that particular segment of that employee or consumer population. I can't think of a better tool to use on your road to becoming an employer of choice for people with disabilities and their families.

If you are still having a little difficulty understanding the difference between affinity and support groups, consider the topics of their conversations. Support groups might discuss medications, research, or treatments. Typical conversations in affinity groups might revolve around work-related assistive technology, best practices for speaking to one's manager about a disability, or how to assist the recruiting department with an on-campus initiative to recruit new grads with disabilities. Sharing that kind of information can enhance productivity and overall employee engagement.

It's not just the employees within the groups who benefit. "Beyond acknowledging the unique challenges that people with disabilities face in the workplace, and the additional responsibilities that parents of children with special needs may have, the group raises awareness among all of our people about the needs and talent of people with disabilities," says Barbara Wankoff, Director of Workplace Solutions for KPMG. "The group also provides resources, information, and education that go out to the people within the network as well as all of our employees, so that people can better understand and support all of our members." That support from co-workers is invaluable. "Creating this level of awareness is so important," says Dana Foote, Audit Partner & Co-Chair of KPMG's Disability Network. "It helps people to see that their fellow co-workers may have additional demands on their lives."

Awareness benefits everyone within an organization. "Individual members have told us how appreciative they are," says Ms. Wankoff. "They see that KPMG has acknowledged their special needs and unique challenges, which makes them feel included in the KPMG culture. That translates into more productivity and increased morale, not just for the one individual, but for all of their colleagues who see that we acknowledge and recognize the needs of individuals. Everybody is an individual: people appreciate knowing that no matter their need, they may be recognized and supported by this firm."

Affinity groups may help provide your employees with even more than recognition and support. WalMart's affinity group helped that company create its emergency evacuation plan. "They looked at our layout of buildings," says Crosby Cromwell, Manager of Disability Markets for WalMart. "They created buddy plans, and recommended evacuation chairs in all of our buildings in case elevators failed."

Good Business

Affinity groups obviously help your employees. They should help your company in a more direct manner, too, by having initiatives that tie back to business goals. Cisco relies on the members of its resource group to assist with recruiting. "They also help us with a different sort of outreach, by ensuring that our products are accessible," says Marilyn Nagel, Director of Inclusion and Diversity for Cisco Systems, Inc. Isn't that a great idea? By using employee resource groups as focus groups, your company will save money (focus groups can be very expensive). More importantly, you're saying that you get it—that people with disabilities are your employees *and* your customers. What a great statement.

➲ **Positive Perspectives:** Redefining Accessibility

"Our partner network, Access Alliance, is very oriented to our business needs. They've helped us recognize the value of universal accessibility; that it's not just something we do for this one person over here. It's not "them and us." It's people who have acquired a disability, or who have had an accident that leaves them temporarily disabled. It's people in their maturing years, or people coming back from war. It's us: at some point we'll all probably experience some kind of disability in our lives. By broadening the scope of disability and redefining accessibility, we're ensuring that we're there and accessible to all of our customers."

—Marthalee Galeota, Diversity Program Manager, Starbucks

Grow a Group

Employee resource groups work best when they begin organically, when someone in your organization sees a need and plants a seed. Cisco's Disability Action Network grew from grass roots. "They help us determine what we need, and how to get it done," says Marilyn Nagel, Cisco's Director of Inclusion and Diversity. "We provide support and backup. It's not us telling the community what to do—it's them telling us what needs to happen."

All of Microsoft's groups are also employee-started. Some are officially sponsored diversity advisory council groups, and some are social groups. They are organized differently. "Social groups just have to say, 'Hey, I'd love to start a group,'" says Loren Mikola, Microsoft's Disability Inclusion Program Manager. "With diversity advisory council groups, we make sure that they have a board of directors, a good base of employees, and goals that align with our business needs."

That brings up another question to ask when starting a group: what type of group will work best, given your corporate culture and the particular group of people who want to meet?

At Ernst and Young, there are several networks that support the special needs workforce. They are organized differently, depending on the needs of the group. "Our parents' (of children with special needs) group is a traditional affinity group, created so that people can share with each other, support one another, and build community. It breaks out into five or six condition-specific groups," says Lori Golden, AccessAbilities Leader for Ernst and Young. "Our AccessAbilities People Resource Network group is different; it comes together to support systemic change, to figure out answers to issues. We did experiment with organizing it as a traditional affinity group, but didn't get enough interest. I think one of the reasons is that the issues can be very different, depending on the disability. Someone who's blind will probably have very different issues than someone who has a cancer diagnosis."

Different issues can mean different groups. The companies interviewed for this book had groups that focused on issues relating to:

+ Parents of children with special needs

+ Veterans with disabilities

+ People who have mobility disabilities

+ People who are deaf or hard of hearing

+ People who are blind or have low vision

+ Caregivers of adults with disabilities

+ Spouses

+ People who have ADHD

+ Allies of all of the above

Which works best—one group or many? There's no one right answer. If your company has only five affinity groups, you probably won't want three disability-related ones, or you might not have the staff or resources for more than one. On the other hand, I've heard many organizations say that they are more successful when they have more than one group, because the issues can be very different. My recommendation? Start out with one group. Be mindful and keep the lines of communication open. If you start to hear that the group's concerns are weighted too heavily in one direction (more in favor of parents, for example), you may want to ask if the group wants to split, or to consider becoming one umbrella group with multiple sub-groups.

The "Ask"

Work-life professionals often ask me why they're having difficulty getting disability affinity groups started. Sometimes it's due to the messaging. Perhaps employees are mistaking the network for a support group. There are a lot of people who would never attend a support group for any reason. They don't want to air their dirty laundry, especially not in the workplace. Make certain that your messaging clearly identifies your group as an affinity group. Convey that the group's goals will connect with business goals and objectives, to help with recruiting, for example. If you know that the group will serve a certain function (focus group, for example), make that clear, too. In the end, it's all about managing to people's expectations.

There's another reason that groups may have a hard time getting off the ground: disclosure. "Right now our group is split about sixty/forty in favor of parents," says Barbara Wankoff of KPMG. "We think it may be easier for parents to disclose that they have a child with special needs than it is for others to disclose that they have a disability. We believe that with everything we're doing—the very visible communication and the support from leadership—that our employees who have disabilities will feel more and more comfortable in participating and asking questions." Dana Foote sees that happening already: "When we first gave people the opportunity to self-identify, only 97 people declared that they had a disability. Just a year later, we had more than double that number. I don't think we hired hundreds more people with disabilities—we think the increase is because more people felt comfortable self-disclosing their disability. There's been a bit of a culture shift."

Your employees need to know that culture shift is real and permanent. If there's any suspicion that disability is the "flavor of the month," people may not self-identify as having a disability (or a child with special needs), fearing that such a disclosure could work against them in the future.

As the KPMG example above illustrates, communication is key. I recommend sending out a company-wide invitation that says something along these lines: "Do you have, or have you ever had, a disability? Short-term or long-term? Visible or invisible? Do you have a child or other dependent with a disability? A close friend or family member?" By putting it out there for everyone, you're allowing people to self-select. By wording it the way I recommend, you're broadening the scope of the group. An example: at one company there was a woman who as a child had contracted polio; its only long-lasting effect was a slight limp. When she first heard about an affinity group forming, she did not join. It wasn't that she wasn't interested; it was that she didn't identify herself as a person with a disability. To her, polio was something that happened to her years ago. It wasn't until later, when someone mentioned that it was a group that was inclusive of people with all sorts of relationships to disability, that she realized she could be included. Reach out to everyone. You may be surprised who joins the group.

Walgreens used another outreach tool to start a group on its corporate campus. During National Disability Employment Awareness month, it set up tables and screened videos outside the employee cafeteria, then asked people if they'd be interested in receiving updates on disability-related events and information. By combining a celebration and information-sharing with the "ask," Walgreens made people feel comfortable. "Quite a few employees disclosed their disabilities to me at the launch. We have more people with disabilities here on the corporate campus than we thought," says Deb Russell, Manager of Outreach and Employee Services. An added benefit: "I think it will help the company leaders understand that we're impacting a lot more people than we realized."

Growing Smart

Once your group is up and running, what's next? First of all, ensure support. "All of our groups work very closely in partnership with one another," says Cisco's Marilyn Nagel. "More mature groups have been tremendous help to new groups. They partner with each other, publicizing each others' seminars, and such. It really promotes cross-education."

Once you've got a good group organized, start spreading the news. After launching its first chapter, KPMG established nine more local chapters. "We were sure to start one in each of our seven geographic regions," says KPMG's Barbara Wankoff. "A couple of areas actually wanted a second chapter." KPMG publicized the groups at national events, and made sure that people could register for the groups online. "We had over 400 members join in a year, and our website has had over 2,500 hits," says Ms. Wankoff. "We think that's pretty good."

The types and number of groups, whether they're official or not, whether they're global or local—all of these decisions depend on your company. The success of your groups also depends on your company, with corporate culture being the most important factor. Have you demonstrated that you understand and support the needs of people with disabilities? Are you viewed as a welcoming and inclusive employer? If you haven't done a good job of showing your support, your employees aren't going to stand up and say, "That's me, I have a disability (or child with special needs)." How do you make sure that you're sending the right message? We've already discussed some of the ideas—resources and RACs, for instance—but there is more that your company can do that will help your employees achieve their needs for work-life balance at the same time.

Little Things, Big Impact

Little things mean a lot. We hear it over and over from appreciative employees. One seemingly little thing you can do is to create a Disability Champions program. This group is different and separate from an affinity group. It's composed of people who feel strongly about welcoming and supporting people with disabilities. They may not have any personal affiliation, but for whatever reason, they feel an alliance or affinity to the disability community, and want to help. Find ways to identify these people within your company by releasing a company-wide call for allies, or making an announcement at a disability-related "lunch and learn."

Again, make sure that the allies' objectives align with your business goals. For example, Ernst and Young's Abilities Champion Network (which is separate from the AccessAbilities People Resource Network) performs a number of tasks. These volunteers conduct "wheel-throughs" of facilities, and note improvements that need to take place. They ensure that disability-awareness messages and educational materials are woven into local communications, meetings, and events. They liaise with the local community, advocate, and organize disability-awareness events. All of these undertakings tie back to their business goals, and demonstrate Ernst and Young's support for the disability community.

Your champion group doesn't have to cover as much ground as Ernst and Young's. Many companies' Disability Champions groups focus on supporting events like the Special Olympics, or on partnering with local chapters of disability organizations, like the Multiple Sclerosis Society. I'll bet that one of your business goals relates back to partnerships within your community; let these great volunteers help you work toward that goal.

More Support

Partnerships can also fit into the "little things mean a lot" category. By creating strategic alliances with disability-related non-profit organizations, you can help to support your employees, brand your company as disability-friendly, attract new consumers and potential talent, find answers and resources for disability-related questions and issues, and (of course) give back to the community.

The community can also give back to you. "When we decided to celebrate National Disability Month, we invited various community organizations to participate in an Access Ability Expo," said Marthalee Galeota, Diversity Program Manager for Starbucks. "We wanted to have information that could help us with access issues for people with various disabilities. I asked that each booth include at least one host with a disability (whether visible or not), and that the booths be experiential in nature. It was great: we had people from the MS (Multiple Sclerosis)

Society, from deaf organizations, and blindness organizations. . . . We had a booth that demonstrated a video relay service, and even one that featured a wheelchair that goes up and down stairs." By partnering with the local community, Starbucks learned about innovative products, resources, and solutions.

The event showed Starbucks commitment to the disability community, and the special needs workforce. Onsite events promoting awareness and celebrating disability rights can help you to get the word out about your disability-friendly culture. Consider these dates when organizing next year's events calendar:

July 26th—The Anniversary of the American with Disabilities Act

Many advocates fought long and hard for the passage of this landmark civil rights legislation. It's a great day to celebrate and to inform people about the law, which prohibits discrimination against individuals with disabilities in employment, public services, public accommodations, transportation, and telecommunications.

December 3rd—International Day of People with Disability

Sanctioned by the United Nations, this day recognizes the achievements and contributions of people with disabilities. Use this day to promote positive images of people with disabilities, and to encourage awareness about the benefits of a truly inclusive society.

October—National Disability Employment Awareness Month

This Congress-designated month has been celebrated since 1945. The Office of Disability Employment Policy (ODEP) provides activities and materials that acknowledge the employment needs and contributions of individuals with all types of disabilities. Many organizations and communities celebrate it simply as "Disability Awareness Month."

Disability Mentoring Day

A great opportunity for your company, this day-long enterprise provides students with disabilities with hands-on career exploration, and provides you with a window into their world—and a possible new recruit! It takes place every year on the third Wednesday of October (as part of National Disability Employment Awareness Month), and is organized by the American Association for People with Disabilities. Check out www.dmd-aapd.org for more information.

More!

Sometimes states or local municipalities will have their own awareness-raising months; in 2008 the governor of Indiana declared March "disability awareness month." Specific cultures may have other dates: February was recently designated as Jewish Disability Awareness month. Specific disabilities also have months dedicated to awareness and information, e.g., May is Mental Health Month and April is Autism Awareness Month. How to keep on top of all of this information? Let your non-profit partners help you. Let them know that you want to be active in the community. "With partnerships, there's a sharing that goes back and forth. They learn what we're doing, and we learn what they're doing. They also let us know what's coming down the pike," says Starbucks Ms. Galeota. "For example, when we talked to the National Federation of the Blind about our new Braille and large print beverage brochure, we found out about the release of a new coin commemorating the work of Louis Braille, and then could add that information to our Braille literacy celebration."

> ⟳ **Inspiration & Innovation: A Celebration of Ability**
>
> *"We do like to have something special in October. This year, we released Braille and large print beverage brochures to our U.S. stores. We worked with national organizations to get input on the documents, had a person who is blind proofread them, and contracted with a manufacturer who was also fully blind. We like to look at things end to end, and try to touch every piece."*
>
> —Marthalee Galeota, Diversity Program Manager, Starbucks

But how exactly do these celebrations and groups help to provide work-life balance? To begin with, they promote understanding and awareness of the unique needs of the special needs workforce, which can translate into support. How? Let's say that a manager has two employees. The first one comes to her and says, "I have a little baby, and really need to talk to you about flextime." Another employee approaches her and says, "I need to talk to you about flextime. I'm having childcare issues with my son, he's fourteen and has autism. . . ." Most managers understand the needs of parents with infants. But without any awareness of disability, this fictional manager might dismiss the second request, thinking, "Your kid's fourteen. Get over it." If that same manager has learned about the different responsibilities of parents of children with special needs, she might understand that exceptional childcare often gets more difficult as a child ages, and that the mother's request is completely valid. The work-life groups, informational events, and partnerships with disability organizations that provided the manager with information may also offer resources that can help her employee with this difficult work-life balance issue.

The last example not only showed how a manager might support a specific work-life balance situation, but illustrated several key pieces of the support puzzle:

- In order to support your employees, you must understand their needs.

- You must let them know that you encourage work-life balance, and appreciate its complexity.

- If you can offer them valuable resources, even better.

I personally feel that no matter the time or circumstance, no one, and no company, can succeed alone. Your company can provide the support and encouragement that make a real difference in your employees' lives—and in turn, the success of your company.

CHAPTER EIGHT

Make Waves—
The Impact

Whether you prefer wide, sandy beaches or wild, craggy coastlines, the beauty of the shore is inescapable, as is the power of the ocean. It's this power which pounds pebbles into sand and creates hidden coves in formidable headlands. Whether it's the gentle, day-after-day action of soft swells, or the crash of mighty breakers, the ocean's waves impact and change the land.

When you choose to employ and support the special needs workforce, you change the landscape of your company, creating safe harbors and wide open vistas. Your actions make waves which impact your workforce, your culture, and your bottom line. But don't take it from me. Listen to the corporate giants who have found that the simple act of inclusion has changed their companies, and sometimes, their worlds.

Transforming the Workforce

It's been my experience that most people with disabilities, especially cognitive disabilities, live lives of isolation. . . . We knew that it (employment) would enrich their lives. If you go there (to Walgreens' Anderson, South Carolina, distribution center) today, you'll see people who didn't talk and would avert their eyes, who will now actively engage you, greet you, and invite you to their workstations. Now they go to the ribs place with team members after work. They have a whole new life. Now that's something we'd hoped for, but what is different is the impact it's had on the "typically able." People with disabilities don't expect charity, they don't expect pity, and they expect to be treated as people. By engaging them, we're the ones who have been changed. There's something about the experience that evokes all that is good. That's what we see among the typically able. When you go there . . . you'll see how people treat each other: **there's more patience, more understanding, more teamwork, more sense of purpose.** It is an overwhelming experience.

—Randy Lewis, Senior Vice President, Walgreens

That's the exciting part about this work; it has the opportunity to circle back and augment this overall issue of people being different, having different abilities. **It also helps to get people past their own barriers.** It can be something as simple as talking to a person who uses a wheelchair, but it helps us to get over our own insecurities, makes us better people, more open and confident. It's intangible but very impactful, and will further strengthen a culture that is already inclusive and very supportive of diversity.

—Ann Andreosatos, North America Region, People with
Disabilities Leader, Proctor & Gamble

With respect to a healthy workforce, **when we are well and good to each other, it's part of our human nature to pass that along.**

—Robin M. Nagel, MS, CDMS, Integrated Disability
Management, Kaiser Permanente

Engaging Employees

It starts at the top. I recently took my little sister as my date to the Chairman's Award, which honors people who give to the community; it's not a disability-related event by any stretch. I was being honored for my community involvement with Special Olympics (for my sister) and the National Multiple Sclerosis Society (for myself). At this dinner, Tim Flynn, our chairman, came out and offered his hand to my sister and escorted her up to the stage so she could take a picture with me. She was just beaming, walking hand in hand with him. It was such a minor act, but so important to me; I almost get teary-eyed even now. That's the level of commitment at the top of this organization, and that filters down to the people. It's the "walk the walk" behind our culture.

I'm pregnant and due at the end of May. I found out a couple of weeks ago that my baby has a congenital diaphragmatic hernia, which will require immediate surgery after he's born. I was planning on taking a short maternity leave . . . obviously it'll be different. If he survives, which I'm positive he will, he'll require some extra attention; he'll be in ICU for a pretty extended period of time. The level of support I've received has been absolutely amazing. Other partners have offered to take on my responsibilities while I'm gone, the network has been great. Shaun Kelly, the co-chair of my network, gave me a personal call. He's third in command of our firm; that's the level of support I feel.

When I'm down, like with this experience, or with an episode with my MS (Multiple Sclerosis), I've always felt so supported; and so, when the firm is in need, or there's a big special project that requires extra time, whatever the case may be, **I feel the need to support them even more than I normally would, because it's a give and take; it's a partnership.** Their help for me drives me to do more and to do better for them.

—Dana Foote, Audit Partner & Co-Chair of the
Disability Network, KPMG

Creating Better Managers

The best way to manage is to know each person as an individual . . . this building (the distribution center in Anderson, South Carolina) teaches you that. I see you as an individual, you see me as an individual. We're all unique. In that way, we can all do the job even with different needs, different desires and different abilities. This is a good way to do business.

—Randy Lewis, Senior Vice President, Walgreens

Establishing an Inclusive Environment

Sometimes people ask, "Do you have specific positions targeted to people with disabilities?" No, we don't. We have positions targeted for people. If that person is qualified, they'll get the job. Whatever accommodation is needed, they'll get it, so they can do their best work. **We appreciate the intellectual horsepower. Being in a wheelchair, using an interpreter, a synthesizer or Braille display; those are all secondary.**

—Loren Mikola, Disability Inclusion, Program Manager, Microsoft

This may sound cliché but it's true: **hiring people with disabilities hasn't changed our culture. It *is* our culture.** We've been at this for quite some time: when the ADA was being discussed, one of our senior executives actually got on a company plane and talked to other corporations, saying, "This isn't a bad thing. It should be welcomed." Back in the day, we had the "McJobs" program, where we partnered closely with organizations that supported people with (mostly intellectual) disabilities, and placed them in our restaurants bussing tables. After a while, our franchisees were doing quite well hiring people with disabilities. "McJobs" actually went away. That was really good news; people went for it without a "program."

—Kevin Bradley, Director of Diversity Initiatives, McDonald's

Making a Better Product

Years ago, **an employee with a disability actually affected the development of a product.** This employee, who was deaf, couldn't hear the audio clips included in ENCARTA, our online encyclopedia. He put a good case together, and convinced the product group to close-caption all the audio sections. It's still the only encyclopedia today that is close-captioned.

—Emily McKeon, Diversity Marketing Manager, Microsoft

We have an accessibility team within our engineering organization that's tapped to ensure that products and services are accessible to people with disabilities. One of the first certified engineers with a disability, who is blind, happens to be on that team. I think that makes a huge difference for us, not only as a commitment to our customers, but as a reminder that **our workforce can help us to relate to all of our customer bases.**

—Marilyn Nagel, Director of Inclusion and Diversity, Cisco Systems, Inc.

People with disabilities are active and informed consumers who have unique insights/expertise about how healthcare works and can be improved. Neglecting to have people with disabilities in healthcare companies is akin to not having women inform the strategy, products, and customer interface approach at a beauty supply company like L'Oréal.

—Deborah Dagit, Vice President and Chief Diversity Officer, Merck & Co., Inc.

Improving Service

By building an infrastructure to keep our workforce working safely and productively, **we're erasing the obstacles that fragment efforts to promote total health in our delivery of patient care.**

—Robin M. Nagel, MS, CDMS, Integrated Disability Management, Kaiser Permanente

Learning from Colleagues

We've learned from our external relationships. We've benchmarked off Wachovia, IBM, Proctor & Gamble, and other corporate partners. We've had great conversations with Walgreens that definitely impact the dialogue and conversation, which goes back to **improving the way we do business for customers and associates with disabilities.**

—Crosby Cromwell, Manager of Disability Markets, WalMart

Attracting New Clients and Partners

Employing people with disabilities has positively impacted us in several ways:

One: **it's enhanced our ability to partner with new clients.** Those partners who also embrace hiring and supporting people with disabilities believe in working with Adecco, and see us as a critical partner for their staffing needs.

Two: through our partnerships with national organizations, the perception of our company has gained a great deal of value: **we're seen as an employer of choice to the disability community.**

Three: we get calls on a weekly basis from organizations who want to partner with us. **They see Adecco as a valuable resource** for employing people with disabilities."

—William Rolack, Diversity Manager, Adecco

Doing Better Business

At McDonald's we never hesitate to tell another corporation that hiring people with disabilities is not charity, it's not a "nice" thing to do, but a smart thing to do for your business. There are fifty-four million people with disabilities at best guess: we actually quadruple that number—they have brothers and sisters, mothers and fathers, teachers, and friends. As a disability-friendly company **that's a lot of money on the table. It's a very valuable consumer market.**

—Kevin Bradley, Director of Diversity Initiatives, McDonald's

Strengthening Community (and Consumer) Support

People definitely notice when you employ people with disabilities. I notice. A young lady who uses a scooter works at a FedEx/Kinko's up the street. I go there because of her. I may pay a little more money, but it's worth it to me, because they're giving her a chance. We see that, too. **Shareholders and customers want to know what you're doing in the community, what you're giving back.**

—Stephen M. Wing, Director of Workforce Initiatives,
CVS Caremark

When we opened the building in South Carolina, we got a lot of national press. After NBC aired a piece, the response on our 800 (consumer relations) number was the largest amount we'd ever had in relation to any press event. We had over a thousand contacts—emails and calls—in just the first week after the story. It was all positive; "I have a family member or someone I care about with a disability," or **"I don't know anyone with a disability, but because you're doing this, I'm going to shop at Walgreens."** It was a huge shock to everyone in the company. It wasn't part of our motivation to attract this attention, but a wonderfully surprising outcome."

—Deb Russell, Manager of Outreach and
Employee Services, Walgreens

Altering the Larger Landscape

Our culture and practices have always supported employees with disabilities. But we can do more. Fully supporting employees who deal with disabilities is complex, yet rich with opportunities to make the culture more inclusive for all employees. **By making an invisible issue visible,** we are raising the bar. We hope to do our part to show the world that supporting people with disabilities is simply a normal part of doing business.

—Ann Andreosatos, North America Region People with
Disabilities Leader, Procter & Gamble

We try to lead by example. From a business to business perspective, when we talk to our suppliers, we let them know that we're very inclusive, we have these values as an organization, and we love to do business with people who have similar values.

—Kevin Bradley, Director of Diversity Initiatives, McDonald's

I know that when customers go in our store and there's a person with an intellectual disability working, the behavior between the baristas—the modeling that happens—has helped customers to become more understanding and appreciative. I've seen the same thing with partners who are deaf. In one of our stores in another country, an elderly gentleman went every day to the same store and got the same drink. One day he went in, and there was a new barista there who was deaf. He was taken aback. Another person took his order, but the person who was deaf introduced herself. The gentleman got his drink and walked off, and then slowly walked back. He said, "Now, I'm coming in tomorrow to get the same drink, and I want to know how to sign my drink." **I do think it makes a difference, and I think it's like giving visibility to disability. It's about making those human connections with people,** which is what Starbucks is all about.

—Marthalee Galeota, Diversity Program Manager, Starbucks

Changing the World

When Randy [Lewis] made the decision to do this, it was because he wanted to change the employment rate of people with disabilities. From early on, we realized that at Walgreens we can only influence 230,000 jobs, too little to make a big dent in society. **Our goal now is to educate companies all over the world, to show them how to do this.** Whatever we learn is education for everybody else, and we're happy to share.

—Deb Russell, Manager of Outreach and
Employee Services, Walgreens

We've been doing this so long that it is just part of our culture now. In certain areas of the company, particularly outside of the Americas and the U.K., I think that the growth and increase in visibility of employees with disabilities and IBM's inclusion in general opens other IBMers' eyes; not only about how to make the workplace more inclusive, but from a business perspective it gets people thinking about other consumers, executives, clients etc. who have disabilities and who participate in the workforce, as well as in commerce in general. **It creates a broader awareness, and makes people rethink the size of the world.**

—John Evans, IBM Human Ability & Accessibility Center, IBM

We're big supporters of the Olympics, and also the Paralympics. At first we were only featuring Olympic athletes on our cups, bags, and tray liners, then started featuring Paralympic athletes as well. **We sent out a global casting call, so people could send in a story about a person in a wheelchair who climbs mountains. When it gets to that point, that's a good thing.**

—Kevin Bradley, Director of Diversity Initiatives, McDonald's

In another country you might work with someone building a store who may not be as eager or interested, or understand the value or benefit of getting into a store without having to use steps. I think that as a company you can have an influence. It's the same with contracts, saying, "If you're going to design a website, we want it to be accessibly designed." One of the very positive aspects of working in a larger company is that **you can have a really positive impact on the world. If we just incorporate and integrate accessibility features within our natural design, they will ultimately benefit everyone.**

—Marthalee Galeota, Diversity Program Manager, Starbucks

Demonstrating the Power of Inclusion

At a shareholder meeting last year, after a lot of bad news in light of the economy, we showed the video of our employees with disabilities in South Carolina. Those employees talked about what it means for them to be working in this environment. A shareholder stood up after that video, and said, "I came here to tell you I was going to sell all my shares in Walgreens; but now I'm going to buy more stock." **That's the power of this issue on the bottom line.**

—Deb Russell, Manager of Outreach and
Employee Services, Walgreens

Changing the Face of Disability, Worldwide

In Mumbai, India, IBM partners with The Victoria Memorial School for the Blind, providing the impetus (and the software) for the school to open a computer center.

IBM has also partnered with the Mexican government and Telmex, a major telecommunications company, to create a technology assistance program that integrates student and adults with disabilities into educational and workplace environments.

CHAPTER NINE

Grab Your Towel and Go — Next Steps

T IME to get in the water. You may feel like waiting until the sun's out, or the water's warmer, or you've had a few more lessons, but don't wait. The time is now. Though I've been asking you to "dive in," it's okay if you want to wade in. But don't delay just because you feel like you're not ready. Start getting ready—suit up and grab your towel.

Wading In

You may feel a bit overwhelmed. It's okay. Don't feel like you have to do all of this at once. Instead, start taking baby steps toward your goal—that of being an employer of choice for the special needs workforce. Your first step? Go back to the beginning. Bring together your key-stakeholders from Diversity, Work-Life, Human Resources, and any other folks who might play a critical role in the development of this initiative, such as Facilities, Legal, or Communications. Take a look at every chapter in the book, and identify the people in your organization who are responsible for the departments or functions identified. Who's in charge of recruiting? Of training? Get the picture? This book has created the platform from which to start.

Once you've identified your key stakeholders, I recommend scheduling a half-day session to meet as a team for the purpose of conducting an internal assessment. Ask the participants to come prepared to discuss their interests, concerns, and past experiences (with your organization or another) relative to supporting the special needs workforce. Ask them to share both successes and failures. Let them know that you truly want to hear every experience, no matter how insignificant it may seem to them. Let everyone put all of their ideas, needs, and hopes on the table, ensuring everyone that "what's said in Vegas stays in Vegas."

Use this book. Formulate a strategic plan that allows you to pursue your low-hanging fruit opportunities while accommodating any identified areas of risk. Keep in mind that corporate culture will play a crucial role, not only in the programs, projects, and initiatives you roll out, but in how you present them. Come together in the decision-making process. As a cohesive, cross-functional team, you can better recognize your corporate culture as it relates to this segment of your employee population, and decide what will work best within your organization.

Team Diving

In order to create an entirely welcoming environment, your team must be able to see the entire picture. In other words, don't let team members skip the chapter on recruiting just because they work in training. Teamwork can save you from a potential disconnect, but only when the entire team works together to connect all of the dots. If each opportunity or potential concern is not explored thoroughly, the team may mistakenly dive into the shallow end of the pool.

Uncover the Opportunities

Once you've completed this process and have seen the entire pool all the way to the bottom, you'll most likely uncover myriad possibilities. Many of them may already exist within your organization. Grab your towel, kick off, and take advantage of those opportunities that are just waiting for you and your team to explore.

Opportunity *is* knocking. An untapped workforce is standing at the doorstep. A workforce that is dedicated, productive, and loyal. A workforce that performs high-quality work, creatively troubleshoots problems, innovates new solutions, and provides out-of-the-box perspectives. Now that you know what the special needs workforce can do for you and your organization, open the door, and welcome them in. For your company, it will mean increased productivity and profitability, but for the employees you serve, it will mean the world.

Organizations, Resources, and Websites

The American Association for the Advancement of Science (AAAS)
202-326-6400   www.aaas.org

AAAS is an international non-profit organization dedicated to advancing science around the world. ENTRY POINT! offers internship opportunities for students with disabilities in science, engineering, mathematics, computer science, and some fields of business. AAAS also publishes a Resource Directory of Scientists and Engineers with Disabilities, which lists professionals with disabilities holding at least a bachelor's degree in a science, technology, engineering, or mathematics field.

The American Association of People with Disabilities (AAPD)
800-840-8844 V/TTY   www.aapd.com

The country's largest cross-disability membership organization, AAPD provides a vast array of information and resources, and hosts Disability Mentoring Day.

AARP
www.aarp.org

The nation's largest membership organization for people 50+, AARP's mission is to enhance the quality of life for all as we age, leading positive social change and delivering value to members through information, advocacy and service. Its website contains information about a variety of age-related subjects, and lists business points of contacts.

Adaptive Environments (AE)
617-695-1225   www.adaptenv.org

The lead organization in the international Universal Design movement, Adaptive Environments is a non-profit organization that promotes design that works for everyone across the spectrum of ability and age.

The Alliance for Technology Access (ATA)
707-778-3011, 707-778-3015 TTY   www.ataccess.org

A national network of community-based resource centers, product developers, vendors, service providers, and individuals, the ATA provides technology-related information and support services to children and adults with disabilities and functional limitations.

The Disability and Business Technical Assistance Center (DBTAC)
800-949-4232 V/TTY   www.adata.org

The Disability and Business Technical Assistance Center (DBTAC) is a national network of 10 regional DBTAC: ADA Centers that provide services for up-to-date information, referrals, resources, and training on the Americans with Disabilities Act (ADA).

DisabilityInfo
DisabilityInfo.gov

This website provides quick and easy access to comprehensive information about disability programs, services, laws and benefits. Topics include:
+ Americans with Disabilities Act (ADA)
+ Fair Housing rights

- Social Security Disability Benefits
- Special education

The site also lists (some) disability resources by state.

Easter Seals
800-221-6827, 312-726-4258 TTY   www.easterseals.com

Easter Seals offers a variety of workforce development services for job-seekers with disabilities, including special programs for older workers and returning veterans with disabilities. It provides job readiness training and job placement services, and in some cases offers continuing on-the-job support, occupational and industry-based skills training, and assistive technology services.

Hire Heroes USA (HHUSA)
866-915-HERO (886-915-4376)   www.HireHeroesUSA.org

The HHUSA program focuses on the career placement of Operation Iraqi Freedom and Operation Enduring Freedom veterans, specializing in the placement of those injured or with any level of disability. HHUSA serves veterans from all branches of the military: Army, Navy, Air Force, Marines, National Guard, Reservists, and Coast Guard. A mission-focused 501(c)(3) not-for-profit program, HHUSA matches the career interests, qualifications, and transferable skills of veterans with the needs of hiring companies, and does so at no cost to either party.

U.S. Department of Labor Veterans' Employment and Training Service
202-693-4700   www.HireVetsFirst.gov

Sponsored by the U.S. Department of Labor, this comprehensive website offers resources and information for veterans and companies interested in hiring vets.

The Job Accommodation Network (JAN)

800-526-7234, 800-ADA-WORK (800-232-9675) *in the United States*

877-781-9403 TTY *in the United States*

304-293-7186 *outside the United States*

www.jan.wvu.edu

> A collaborative effort of the U.S. Department of Labor Office of Disability Employment Policy (ODEP) and the International Center for Disability Information at West Virginia University, JAN provides free consulting services for all employers, regardless of the size of an employer's workforce. Services include one-on-one consultation about all aspects of job accommodations, including the accommodation process, accommodation ideas, product vendors, referral to other resources, and ADA compliance assistance.

National Business and Disability Council (NBDC) at Abilities!

516-465-1516   www.nbdc.com

> NBDC offers resources for employers seeking to integrate people with disabilities into the workplace and companies seeking to reach them in the consumer marketplace. Job posting and a national résumé database are among the many services it provides to its members.

National Council on Disability (NCD)

202-272-2004, 202-272-2074 TTY   **www.ncd.gov**

> NCD is an independent federal agency that provides advice to the President, Congress, and executive branch agencies to promote policies, programs, practices, and procedures that guarantee equal opportunity for all individuals with disabilities and empower individuals with disabilities to achieve economic self-sufficiency, independent living, and inclusion and integration into all aspects of society.

The National Council on Independent Living (NCIL)
877-525-3400, 202-207-0340 TTY   www.ncil.org

The National Council on Independent Living is the longest-running, national cross-disability, grassroots organization run by and for people with disabilities. Under its umbrella are Centers for Independent Living (CILs) and Statewide Independent Living Councils (SILCs). These advocacy-driven organizations are run by and for people with disabilities, and can offer local disability-related information.

The National Disability Institute
202-296-2040   www.ndi-inc.org

The National Disability Institute is a national research and development organization that promotes income preservation and asset development for persons with disabilities and builds healthy financial futures for Americans with disabilities.

National Organization on Disability (NOD)
202-293-5960, 202-293-5968 TTY   www.nod.org

The National Organization on Disability (NOD)'s mission is to expand the participation and contribution of America's 54 million men, women and children with disabilities in all aspects of life. Its website contains information on internship programs, emergency evacuation for people with disabilities, plus resources and referrals to locate qualified workers with disabilities, and much more.

The Office of Disability Employment (ODEP)
866-633-7365   www.dol.gov/odep/

This sub-cabinet level policy agency in the Department of Labor offers resources to both employers and job-seekers, provides links to job-matching/and job posting sites, and offers tips for conducting an accessible interview process. The Employer Assistance Referral Network (EARN) and the Workforce Recruitment Program for College Students with Disabilities (WRP) are both under the ODEP umbrella.

One-Stop Career Centers
877-US2-JOBS (877-872-5627), 877-889-5627 TTY
www.servicelocator.org/   www.careeronestop.org

America's Service Locator connects individuals to employment and training opportunities available at local One-Stop Career Centers. The website provides contact information for a range of local work-related services, including unemployment benefits, career development, and educational opportunities. CareerOneStop is a U.S. Department of Labor-sponsored website that offers career resources and workforce information to job seekers, students, businesses, and workforce professionals to foster talent development in a global economy.

The United Nations (UN)
www.un.org/disabilities

This web page provides information about the rights and dignity of persons with disabilities around the world, and how the UN is protecting and promoting these rights.

United States Access Board
800-872-2253, 800- 993-2822 TTY   www.access-board.gov

The Access Board is an independent federal agency devoted to accessibility for people with disabilities and is a leading source of information on accessible design. The Board develops and maintains design criteria for the built environment, transit vehicles, telecommunications equipment, and for electronic and information technology. It also provides technical assistance and training on these requirements and on accessible design and continues to enforce accessibility standards that cover federally funded facilities.

The U.S. Business Leadership Network (USBLN)
www.usbln.org

The only national disability organization led by business, for business, USBLN supports development and expansion of 53 BLN affiliates in 31 states. These organizations recognize and promote best practices in hiring, retaining, and marketing to people with disabilities. Using a business-to-business approach, they provide career fairs, mentoring, and internship programs, as well as training programs for employers. Many of the employers interviewed for this book are members.

U.S. Department of Justice, Civil Rights Division, Disability Rights Section
800-514-0301, 800-514-0383 TTY
800-514-0301 (Americans with Disabilities Act (ADA) Information Hotline)
www.ADA.gov

The Disability Rights Section protects the rights of persons with disabilities under Titles I, II, and III of the Americans with Disabilities Act. Its website provides updated information on disability rights issues, and links to other disability-related government websites. The ADA Business Connection (a website section) offers information for businesses including ADA publications, ADA *Business Briefs*, design standards, and ADA regulations.

The U.S. Equal Employment Opportunity Commission (EEOC)
800-669-4000, 800-669-6820 TTY   www.eeoc.gov

The U.S. Equal Employment Opportunity Commission makes equal employment opportunity policy, approves most litigation, and conducts EEOC enforcement litigation under Title VII of the Civil Rights Act of 1964, the Equal Pay Act (EPA), the Age Discrimination in Employment Act (ADEA), and the Americans with Disabilities Act (ADA). Its website provides information about Title I (employment) of the ADA.

U.S. Paralympics

www.usparalympics.org

U.S. Paralympics, a division of the U.S. Olympic Committee, is dedicated to becoming the world leader in the Paralympic sports movement. It promotes excellence in the lives of people with physical disabilities through education, sports programs and partnerships with community organizations, medical facilities, and government agencies.

Web Accessibility Initiative (WAI)

617-253-2613   www.w3.org/WAI

WAI is a non-profit organization with global reach that develops strategies, guidelines, and resources to make the web accessible to people with disabilities.

The World Institute on Disability (WID)

510-763-4100, 510-208-9493 TTY   www.wid.org

A public policy center organized by and for people with disabilities, the World Institute on Disability's work focuses on problems and issues, including employment, that directly affect people's ability to live full and independent lives.

Index

A

Abilities, Inc./Business Advisory Council, 21

Ability champions, 70

absentee rates, 2, 18, 80

AccessAbilities™, 35, 60

accessibility
  guidelines (physical), 50, 71, 103 ,125
  website, 29, 50, 84, 87

accommodations, 60–68
  benefits of, 56
  centralized budgeting, 67
  costs of, 55, 66–68
  handling requests, 65
  Reasonable Accommodation Committee (RAC), 62–66

Adaptive Environments (AE), 121

Adecco, 11, 15, 19, 20–22, 32, 54–55, 58

adult bullying, 32

Alliance for Technology Access, 121

American Association for the Advancement of Science (AAAS), 26, 120

American Association of People With Disabilities (AAPD), 25, 120

American Management Association, 8

Americans with Disabilities Act (ADA), 12, 38–39, 42, 50, 56–57, 62, 71
  Accessibility guidelines (ADAAG), 84

Andreosatos, Ann, 28, 60, 86, 108, 114

assistive technology, 50, 59–60

Association of Retired Persons (AARP), 7, 15, 19, 120

Australian Employers Network of Disability, 2–3

B

baby boom generation, 6

Blue Ocean Strategy, 19

Bradley, Kevin, 15, 38, 53, 110, 114, 115–116

Braille, 10, 28, 46

C

Carolina Fine Snacks, 3

Cisco Systems, Inc., 38, 86, 97–98, 101

cognitive disabilities, 18, 47, 61

Colbert, Suzanne, 2–3

communication, visual, 62

company loyalty, 19

corporate culture, 35, 58–59

Cromwell, Crosby, 25, 72, 90, 97, 112

cultural competency, 31–33

CVS Caremark, 15, 19, 26–27

D

Dagit, Deborah, 18, 37, 91, 111,

Disability and Business Technical Centers (DBTACs), 121

disability awareness events, 104–105

disability etiquette, 31–33, 41–43, 45–52

Disability Mentoring Day, 25, 104–105, 120

Disability Recruitment Partnerships, Events, and Activities (report), 20–21

DisabilityInfo.gov, 121

discretionary spending, 3

diversity among and within disabilities, 9, 10, 47–48

Down Syndrome, 4, 31, 83

E

Easter Seals, 24–25, 122

Ehlers-Danlos Syndrome, 12

emergency preparedness, 32, 50, 62, 71–73, 97, 124

Employee Assistance Providers (EAP), 78–79

employee benefits, 74–81
  disability, 75–76
  health insurance, 75–76
  Health Insurance Empowerment
    Seminars, 77
  letters of medical necessity, 76
  life insurance, 75
  need for guidance, 74–75, 79–81
employee resources, 82–93, 96–97
employee traits, 1–2
Employer Assistance Referral Network
  (EARN), 23
employer of choice, 8, 81,
Ernst & Young, 35, 38, 60, 70–71, 77–78,
  89, 98
"ethical enthusiasts", 16
Evans, John, 16, 25, 59, 60, 115

F-G
federal employees, 14
federal government (as employer), 20
Foote, Dana, 42, 47, 63, 97, 100, 109
Galeota, Marthalee, 70, 98, 103, 105, 114,
  116
Gallaudet University, 28
Gartner, Mike, 28
Generation X, 8
Generation Y, 8
Golden, Lori, 35, 38, 60, 71–72, 77–78,
  89–90, 95, 99
Grandin, Dr. Temple, 18

H-I
Helen Keller Institute, 54–55, 59
hidden disabilities, 48
Hire Heroes USA, 24, 122
HireVetsFirst.gov, 24, 122
IBM, 12, 16, 25, 59, 60, 90, 116
  Global Building Accessibility Checklist,
    71
inclusion, 10
innovation, 2, 9, 16–18

J-K
Job Accommodation Network (JAN), 55,
  68, 123
Kaiser Permanente, 11, 68–69, 89
Kaplan, Shelley, 17, 25, 35, 37, 46, 60–61, 64
Katz, Linda, 54–55, 58, 59
Kim, W. Chan, 20
KPMG, 11, 42, 47, 62, 63, 77, 96, 101

L-M
language, 43–44
Lewis, Mary E., 69
Lewis, Randy, 107–108, 109–110
"lunch and learn", 88, 102
Mauborgne, Renée, 20
McDonald's, 11, 15, 38, 39–40, 53
McKeon, Emily, 110–111
Merck & Co., 18, 37, 91, 111
Meyer, Karen, 38
Microsoft, 38, 41–42, 66, 90, 98
Mikola, Loren, 38, 41–42, 66, 98, 110

N
Nagel, Marilyn, 38, 86, 97–98, 101, 108,
Nagel, Robin, 69, 111
NASA, 26
National Business and Disability Council, 123
National Council on Disability, 32, 123
National Council on Independent Living,
  124
National Disability Employment Awareness
  month, 101, 104–105
National Disability Institute, 124
National Organization on Disability, 8, 124
National Science Foundation, 61

O-P
Obama, Barack, President, 14
Office of Disability Employment Policy
  (ODEP), 22–23, 58, 124
older workers, 2, 4–6, 15, 70
One-Stop Career Centers, 125
organizational readiness, 30

"people first language and philosophy",
42–43
Peterson, Christine M., 19
Pew Research Center, 5
Pizza Hut, 3
Population Reference Bureau, 6
Procter & Gamble, 28, 60, 86

R
recruiting, 2, 100
　interview process, 22
　tools, 27–28, 29
recruiting and retention, 30
relocation issues, 91–93
Rolack, William, 20–21, 112
Russell, Deb, 21–22, 41, 58, 62, 78, 101, 113,
115, 116

S
seizure disorders, 48
service animals, 49–50
signage, 62
Sloane Work and Family Research Network,
95
sneaker wave, 6
social justice, 12
Society for Human Resource Managers
(SHRN), 6, 8, 68, 95
Southeast Disability Business Technical
Assistance Center (DBTAC), 17, 25, 37,
46, 57
Southerland, Rebecca, 19
special needs workforce definition, 4
St. John, Bonnie, 17–18, 45
Stanford, Percil, Dr., 15, 19, 44, 70
Starbucks, 61–62, 70, 98, 103–104, 105
statistics, 13–14, 16, 32, 55, 56, 68, 95
　loyalty and reduced turnover, 3
　older workers, 5–7
　veterans, 23–24

T
tardiness, 3
tax benefits, 7

telecommuting, 60–61
TeleTYpewriters (TTY) (definition), 24
training, 31–53
　customized, 35–40
　experiential, 40, 70–71
　types. 36, 39–40
　what to include, 45–52
　who to train, 33–35

U-V
U.S. Business Leadership Network (USBLN),
24, 126
U.S. Census, 3
U.S. Department of Justice, 126
U.S. Department of Labor, 6, 55, 58, 122
U.S. Internal Revenue Service, 7
U.S. Paralympics, 17–18, 45, 115, 127
United Nations, 125
United States Access Abroad, 125
universal design concepts, 21, 70
U.S. Equal Employment Opportunity Com-
mission, 126
veterans, 14, 23–24, 32
Vocational Rehabilitation Agencies (state),
23

W
Walgreens, 21–22, 41–42, 58–59, 62, 78, 101
WalMart, 20, 25, 29, 72–73, 90, 97
Wankoff, Barbara, 62–64, 77, 96, 100, 102
Web Accessibility Initiative, 127
Wing, Stephen M., 15, 19–20, 26–27, 40, 113
Workforce Recruitment Program for College
Students with Disabilities (WRP), 23
work-life balance, 8, 94–106
World Institute on Disability, 127

The Authors

Nadine O. Vogel

Nadine O. Vogel is Founder and President of Springboard Consulting LLC. Springboard works with national and global firms on how to appropriately support employees who either have a disability, or who have a child or other dependent with special needs, through diversity, work-life, and human resource initiatives. Springboard also enables these firms to successfully market their products and services to this community, now the largest minority market in the world! Springboard also produces the Disability Matters Awards Banquet and Conference which honors those firms that are making great strides in the areas of marketing, work-life, and diversity as it pertains to the special needs population.

Prior to founding Springboard, Nadine held a variety of senior level positions in both corporate America and the non-profit sectors.

Vogel has authored numerous articles and is recognized as a powerful motivational, inspirational speaker. Recognized for her civic and professional activities, Vogel has received many awards and accolades including:

the *NJ BIZ Magazine* 2008 Best 50 Women in Business Award; the Count Me In, 2008 Make Mine a Million $ Business Program Award; the 2007 Howard L. Green Humanitarian Award from the NJ Broadcasters Association; the College of Charleston 2003 Distinguished Alumni Award; the Voices Award 2003—individuals who have made a difference in the community; the Golden Gate University 2002 Alumni Community Service Award; the *Fast Company Magazine* 2002 debut list of "Fast 50" innovators—individuals whose achievements helped change their companies or society; the *Working Mother Magazine* Mothers We Love Top 25 List in 2000, and the magazine's 2000 Mothering That Works Award; and numerous elections to a variety of editions to Who's Who.

Vogel has been featured on NBC News, CNNfn, Lifetime Live on the Lifetime Channel, *Good Day NY,* and Oxygen Television's *Pure Oxygen* program. She is the founder and past president of the board of SNAP, Special Needs Advocate for Parents, a member of the NJN TV Corporate Advisory Committee, a member of the Expert Advisory Committee of United Cerebral Palsy and on the editorial advisory board for *WorkLife Matters Magazine.* She is a member of the College of Charleston Foundation Board and a member of the College of Charleston Department of Communications Professional Advisory Council.

Vogel received an MBA from Golden Gate University in San Francisco, California, and a BS in Industrial Psychology from the College of Charleston in Charleston, South Carolina. She resides in New Jersey with her husband and two daughters, both of whom have special needs.

Cindy Brown

Cindy Brown combines her passion for access with her training and writing expertise. As a trainer and consultant, she travels nationwide, providing training and technical assistance on architectural accessibility and other ADA and access-related issues. She was a team member for two national award-winning disability-related projects: disability-arts organization ARTability, awarded the National Innovation Award by the National State Arts Agencies/National Endowment for the Arts; and the *Access Tempe* brochure, which won the Society for Accessible Travel and Hospitality's 2008 Media Award.

As a writer, Ms. Brown has received awards from the Media Communication Association International (Arizona Chapter), the Screenwriting Conference at Santa Fe, and the Scottsdale Motion Picture/Television Film & Video Festival. She was a reviewer for the book *Design for Accessibility,* produced in partnership with the National Endowment for the Arts, The National Endowment for the Humanities, National Assembly of State Arts Agencies and the John F. Kennedy Center for the Performing Arts. Ms. Brown's regular writing clients include Pearson/Prentice Hall, Edward Sweet and Associates, and *Active Living Magazine.*

Ms. Brown understands disability on a personal level, as someone who lives with Ehlers-Danlos Syndrome. Disabled in 1996, she soon became involved with the disability community, and was presented with the 2004 Mayor's Award from the City of Phoenix Mayor's Commission on Disability Issues, in particular for her work in media and the arts. She and her husband recently moved to Portland, Oregon.